Fire Dragon Feminism

Fire Dragon Feminism

Asian Migrant Women's Tales of Migration, Coloniality and Racial Capitalism

Ee Ling Quah

BLOOMSBURY ACADEMIC
LONDON • NEW YORK • OXFORD • NEW DELHI • SYDNEY

BLOOMSBURY ACADEMIC
Bloomsbury Publishing Plc, 50 Bedford Square, London, WC1B 3DP, UK
Bloomsbury Publishing Inc, 1359 Broadway, 12th Floor, New York, NY 10018, USA
Bloomsbury Publishing Ireland, 29 Earlsfort Terrace, Dublin 2, D02 AY28, Ireland

BLOOMSBURY, BLOOMSBURY ACADEMIC and the Diana logo are trademarks
of Bloomsbury Publishing Plc

First published in Great Britain 2025
Reprinted 2025

A catalogue record for this book is available from the British Library.

Library of Congress Cataloging-in-Publication Data

ISBN: HB: 978-1-3504-4781-3
PB: 978-1-3504-4782-0
ePDF: 978-1-3504-4784-4
eBook: 978-1-3504-4783-7

Typeset by Newgen KnowledgeWorks Pvt. Ltd., Chennai, India
Printed and bound in Great Britain

For product safety related questions contact
productsafety@bloomsbury.com

To find out more about our authors and books visit www.bloomsbury.com
and sign up for our newsletters.

Contents

Figures

1

Introduction: I got into trouble

I got into trouble …

I got into serious trouble when I complained about racism. Trouble that caught me off guard. Trouble that sent shock waves to my already traumatized body. Trouble that I have never encountered in my two decades of work life across three countries. I was blindsided. It was not the outcome I had expected when I wrote that 'fuck you, racism' article. I had hoped that the article (Quah 2020b) exposing my encounters with racism as an Asian queer migrant woman living and working in a predominantly white Australian settler-colonial society would motivate meaningful and courageous anti-racism work. In that tell-it-all article (Quah 2020b), I presented an inventory of racism detailing the everyday, casual, institutional and overt racist encounters and interrelated dominance I have experienced, first as an international 'Asian' student and subsequently, as a gainfully employed 'Asian' woman professional. The article was not simply a complaint of oppressive forces or self-indulgent, attention-grabbing whine about victimization. More than truth-telling and life stories offered by a queer migrant woman of colour researcher, the article was a reorientation of strategy to survive, live on and thrive in the face of constrictive structures. In the article, I polished my anti-coloniality, anti-racism feminist armour further to a shine and gave the restorative and resistance strategy I developed earlier – fire dragon feminism (Quah 2020a) – a more definitive form and purpose. It was a crucial exercise where I reflected upon prolonged exposure to racial violence, navigation of difficult and contradictory emotions in the face of racism, and development of generative feminist tools including feminist rage, queer pessimism and fire dragon feminist hopes while inhabiting in the violence.

I did not expect and could not have anticipated the violent and sinister backlash that exploded after the 'fuck you, racism' article was published. It certainly caught me off guard since the article quickly generated significant interest and positive reviews among supportive readers. The haters, perhaps unsurprisingly, felt threatened and were enraged by the exposé. They attacked two of my credentials: research and teaching that were core to my professional standing. Enabled by colour-blind and seemingly neutral institutional mechanisms set up to maintain status quo of white privilege and minoritized populations' subjugation, they made sure I understood their outrage towards my insubordination and insolence by registering undesirable consequences on my livelihood. The extensive and brutal institutional force of punishing and silencing dissent came quashing down and shattered my othered body, beliefs and hopes into pieces.

Crushed and shaken, I was lucky enough to enter a season of treatment, rest and recovery after the most tormenting year in my twenty-three-year work life. It was then I decided it was time to process what has happened to me since writing that 'fuck you, racism' article and write a sequel of the article. It was time to collect my traumatized self, muster whatever courage I could find within myself and harness my fire dragon feminist superpowers to show up for myself and others who have encountered similar experiences. It was time to make sense of my lived experiences within broader structures of power and inequalities. It was time to write to release the pain and anguish my broken body has come to bear and recentre my sense of self and purpose. It was also time to rejoin the loud and noisy protests of generations of anti-coloniality, anti-racism feminist activists who have come before me. Therefore, here I am, showing up to speak against racism and its deeply interconnected hegemonies including white supremacy, racial capitalism, neoliberalism and patriarchy. Only this time, instead of a fire-blazing, bulldozing 'fuck off, racism!' offense without proper protective armour and survival gears, it is a more calculated and careful '*kindly* fuck off, racism' move. This choreographed strategy, as I have come to realize, is necessary for survival, self-compassion and longevity of fire dragon feminism.

Content warnings and disclaimers

Before proceeding with the book, readers are strongly advised to read the following trigger warnings and disclaimers. The contents of the book may cause discomfort and distress if you have encountered racism, systemic violence, white patriarchy, white liberal feminism, sexism, gender-based violence and other manifestations of subjugation and injustice. For these readers, please have your lifeline and helpline numbers near you as the book may jolt painful memories you have carefully tidied away for a somewhat restored and productive life. The contents may also cause discomfort, dissonance, displaced anger, disproportionate guilt and distress if you find yourself having participated or being complicit in exacting violence, gaslighting victims, whitewashing inequalities, silencing dissent and rationalizing away your involvement. For these readers, there are abundant anti-racism learning resources online and in libraries to consult with, learn from and reflect on.

This book does not seek to represent and generalize lived experiences of Asian migrant populations in white majority settler-colonial societies. Asian is an expansive term, and I adopt the UN's categorization of Asian region comprising forty-eight countries including Central, East, Southeast, South and West Asia (United Nations Statistics Division 2024). There is a wide variety of ethnic and language groups in the geographical region of Asia. It will be unrealistic to claim that stories in this book are representative of the vast diversity of Asian ethnic minority, migrant groups living in white majority settler-colonial societies. I use the term 'Asian' not to flatten differences and ignore heterogeneity of the wide diverse historical, political, economic and sociocultural landscapes of the largest continent in the world. The deliberate reference of 'Asian migrant women' is to illuminate the racializing structures and habits of white dominant societies. I have written earlier (Quah 2020b) about how baffled I was when I first encountered 'Asian food', 'Asian people' and 'Asian culture' after arriving in Australia in my thirties as a PhD international student. Growing up in Singapore and having travelled, worked and lived in the Southeast Asian region, I am deeply appreciative of the vast richness of historical and cultural heritage in the region of Asia. However, my initiation into the white Australian society involved a rude lesson on the conflation of all forty-eight Asian countries and their multiple cultural groups into a single category. Not only is such simplistic reference a display of ignorance towards the multiple cultural heritages an individual may practise because of complex ancestry, heritage and intergeneration migration, but it also reinforces the deep-seated racialization and othering of people from the region of Asia. Differences among multiple cultures, languages, histories and geographies are wilfully reduced, disregarded and disrespected. Asian, together with First Nations, Arab, Muslim and Jewish populations in Australian society have long been othered, marginalized, excluded and misrepresented by the white Anglo-Celtic majority (see, for example, Cowlishaw 2004; Mellor 2006; Loy-Wilson 2014, 2019; Hickey 2016; Khatun 2018; Park 2019; Moreton-Robinson 2020a). The deliberate reference of 'Asian' in this book is therefore to allude to the persistent categorization of humanity with the Western Man as the benchmark of civility and superiority and the other peoples being ranked more inferiorly in lower racial hierarchal orders. It is also used to open up discussions on Asian migrant women's involvements and outcomes in an ongoing racialization process.

Readers are therefore advised to refrain from making generalizations and assumptions but, instead, invited to encounter the contents with an open mind and a curious spirit. Having said that, the lived experiences and life stories in this book are valid and real contributing to the rich archives of migrant stories, especially stories about women from multicultural, multilingual, multifaith migrant backgrounds in Australia. The encounters with oppressive structures of colonialism, racial capitalism, neoliberalism and white patriarchy mentioned in the book may not be quite the same as readers' experiences. However, readers who find the stories familiar and relatable will hopefully find validation in the stories and be assured that their own lived experiences with such oppressive systems are real too. Readers who are privileged enough to not have to deal with everyday racialization and minoritization will hopefully gain some meaningful insights into intersectional struggles with whiteness, xenophobia, racism, heteropatriarchy, misogyny and other forms of systemic violence.

The book is an anti-colonial, anti-racist, intersectional and migrant feminist intervention drawing from lived experiences and ethnographic observations residing and working in a predominantly white settler-colonial society. Its conceptualizations and discussions are anchored in broader scholarly literature on systemic racialized violence and a long history of feminist greats' fearless storytelling and activism. The discussions do not skirt around uncomfortable topics for fear of rousing white guilt, upsetting white comfort and provoking white rage. Instead, the book sets out to expose unjust structures, whitewashing processes and practices, quiet complicity, victim blaming and other violent manifestations of coloniality and racial capitalism in disguise. It is important to note though the book is not one that subscribes to the binary of 'evil oppressor versus weak victim', 'they versus us' and 'white people versus racial minorities'. It is not a project that sets out to create simplistic caricature of evilhood out of white people and those responsible for and complicit in perpetuating racism. It is not a crusade to demonize and crucify white people and turn non-white people into innocent, helpless and powerless victims. The complexity of humanity cannot be reduced to an uncomplicated and unproblematic picture of good and bad and godly and evil. The book is also not an attempt to stir white guilt, beg for white benevolence and evoke sympathy for survivors of racism. Instead, its interpretive and reflective potential invites readers to a space of reflection, connection and inspiration. The book is a loud, careful, fiery, compassionate and hopeful social justice breath of a fire dragon feminist slaying deep-seated, complex structural inequalities and calling for a more just, equitable and sustainable existence.

Acknowledgement of privileges, complicity and responsibilities on occupied Indigenous lands

One of the fundamental ground rules a fire dragon feminist sets out to follow is to constantly reflect upon and acknowledge one's privileges, positionality and participation as one goes about interacting with people, systems and environments and carrying out social justice activism work. When I got into serious trouble with whiteness after my loud protest against racism, I was inevitably upset, scared and shaken by the traumatic punitive outcomes. As if every day violent encounters with racism throughout my migration biography have not already imprinted long-lasting trauma-induced fears, messed up my sense of safety and instilled heightened hypervigilance, the backlash I encountered as a result of the 'fuck you, racism' article sent chilling panic waves all over my shattered body and further crushed my broken spirit. The punishing repercussions resulted in significant implications on multiple aspects of my life from physical health to mental state to emotional well-being to career development to financial expenditures. However, a part of me wondered if I had the right to be loud in protesting against racism and claim victimization by racial injustice. I suffered from not just deep grief over losses associated with the racist attacks but also disenfranchised grief (Robson & Walter 2013) due to my privileged positions. I grieved over the profound sense of loss of trust in communities I interacted with and the sense of betrayal and rejection I experienced at the same time. However, I did not feel I could grieve openly and legitimately, hence the disenfranchised grief I embodied. Who am I to complain about racism when I have been part of a racial majority most of my adult life reaping all kinds of unearned racial benefits in my home country? Who am I to talk about racism when I am now residing on and reaping material gains from lands that remain stolen from dispossessed Indigenous populations? Who am I to make so much noise about racism when I share the same ancestry as past Chinese migrant-settlers who had directly or indirectly involved themselves in British colonization of Indigenous lands and massacres and displacement of Indigenous peoples and went on to endow their descendants including me with intergenerational racial dividends?

Indeed, I am privileged in many ways. I was born and raised in rapidly advancing postcolonial Singapore, eager to prove to the world its economic formidability despite its tiny geographical size as an island city state. Growing up in one of the four well-known booming Asian tiger economies (Hong Kong, South Korea and Taiwan being the other three), promises of progress, improved standard of living and a good future fill my hopeful conscience and gift me a fearless naivety about my ability to succeed and thrive. Upon reflection, only a well-resourced citizen of a highly ranked, wealthy nation where political, economic and social turmoil is not its everyday reality could hold such a taken-for-granted introspection and outlook. In the absence of wars, civil conflicts, natural disasters and economic crises, the day-to-day drive to strive for excellence improve the country's international standing and fly its flag high entered my psyche. Having the space to dream, work for one's dream and believe the dream will come true is itself a significant material privilege. As the descendant of ethnic Chinese migrant-settlers, I grew up as a member of the Chinese ethnic majority population in Singapore and was largely oblivious to the casual and institutional racism my ethnic minority peers encountered and still face in their everyday lives.

Under the British colonial rule from 1819 to 1959, Chinese, Indian, Malay, Javanese, Bugis and Balinese migrants settled in Singapore (Saw 2012). In 1941, my late paternal grandfather migrated to Singapore from China, Fujian 福建 province, Anxi 安溪 county, popularly known as the country's tea capital producing the famous tea, Iron Goddess 铁观音. As the eldest son, my then eighteen-year-old grandfather was

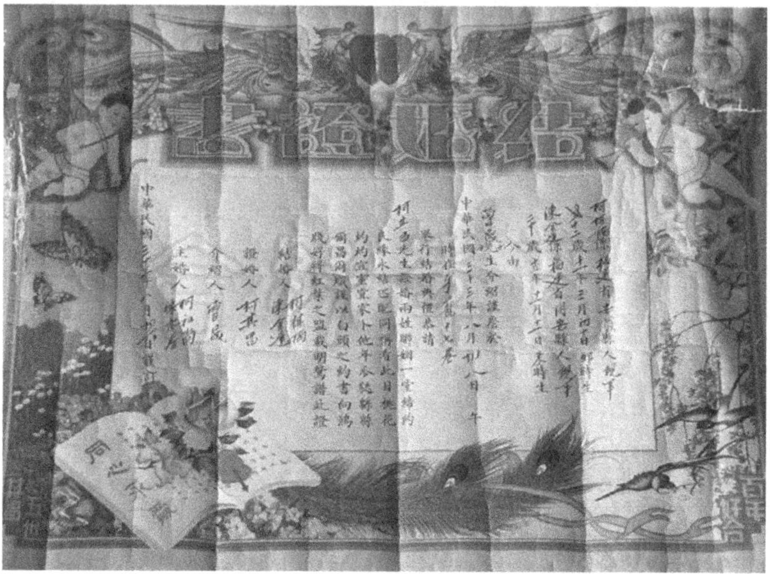

Figure 1.1 Marriage certificate of my paternal grandparents.

the first in the family to take the plunge in joining the wave of early Chinese migrants and enduring a treacherous voyage in a Chinese junk ship to Nanyang 南洋, now known as Singapore. Once settled down earning a meagre income as a 'karang guni man' (colloquial expression of a scrap dealer, rag and bone man) and saving enough passage fare, he paid and arranged for his father and stepbrothers to make the same voyage to Nanyang. My late grandfather's migration journey marked the beginning of Quah's family tree extending its branches in Singaporean society. He and his family quickly took root by working out their livelihood pathways, getting married and raising families. In 1945, my grandfather married my Singapore-born grandmother, a second-generation of Chinese immigrant, also from Fujian province but a different county, Tong An 同安 (see Figure 1.1 for their marriage certificate). Their descendants born and raised in Singapore gradually lost ties with their ancestral lands (see Figure 1.2 for Quah family portrait). My grandfather's migratory story is certainly not unique but emblematic of Chinese migrant-settler population who immigrated to

Figure 1.2 Quah family portrait.

Singapore, a then rapidly developing British colony offering prospective economic opportunities to impoverished populations in the region. The number of Chinese immigrants in Singapore notably increased from 2,069 in 1838–9 to 10,928 in 1849–50 to 95,400 in 1890 to 190,901 in 1895 (Ee 1961: 33). Many of these early migrants came from two coastal provinces, Fujian and Guangdong, 'the poorest and most disrupted areas throughout the nineteenth century' (Kuah 1990: 372), which explains their mass movements down south to seek survival and a better life.

A combination of rapid economic globalization, increasing labour demands, declining fertility rates of local ethnic Chinese populations and state's desire to maintain population ratio of its Chinese, Malay, Indian, Others (CMIO) multiracial model (Yeoh & Lin 2013) led to post-war ethnic Chinese population steadily increasing and making up of 74 per cent of total Singaporean population (Statistic Singapore 2021). As a result, I inherited and benefitted from unearned racial privilege and unlike my ethnic minority Malay, Indian and other ethnic minority peers, I did not grow up at risk of encountering casual and institutional racism. Inundated by official 'multiculturalism' and 'racial harmony' rhetoric in schools and state-controlled television programmes, my racial literacy was almost non-existent. I grew up taking for granted that race, like sex and blood type, was simply a neutral demographic characteristic category that I ticked on forms unquestioningly. I remember I went as far as taking pride in my colour blindness and believing that my lack of race consciousness was a signifier of my 'not racist' upbringing and model citizenship. For the most part of my adult life in Singapore, I did not for a moment consider the possibility that my ethnic minority friends and colleagues exist in rather different parallel realities on the same small, highly manicured and neatly compartmentalized city island. However, reading racial minority Singaporeans' accounts such as Farah Bawany's (2021) autoethnographic article has been especially sobering when their works illuminate lived racialized experiences and embodied racial injuries of non-Chinese minoritized peoples in Singapore.

At the point of writing this book, I have been living and working as a middle-class, highly educated, materially comfortable, culturally and racially marginalized immigrant, queer woman academic for more than a decade on stolen, occupied Indigenous lands in so-called Australia. I acknowledge the Aboriginal and Torres Strait Islander peoples as traditional owners and custodians of my host country and that their sovereignty was never ceded. I acknowledge that I have been reaping privileges and benefits from my economic and queer immigration and participation in racial capitalist systems of existing settler colonial, predominantly white Australian society that continues to subjugate and marginalize Indigenous peoples. I therefore acknowledge my consequent complicity in perpetuating racial violence and injustices against Indigenous Australian populations due to my role as a productive member of white Australian dominant systems. Sharing the same ancestry as early Chinese immigrants in Australia during British colonial period, I am aware that my location as a Chinese immigrant in contemporary Australia means I inhabit in similar spaces where I enjoy privileges and discrimination at the same time (Stephenson 2003). Early Chinese migrant-settlers in Australian settler colony were 'simultaneously victimised by, and implicated in the colonising mission' (Stephenson 2003: 61). Like these early Chinese migrant-settlers, I am not only subjected to white racial superiority but also contribute to global and national racial capitalist expansion projects at the ongoing expense of Indigenous peoples. In addition, I possess nationality privileges as a Singaporean citizen. In the global hierarchy of nations, Singapore occupies a prominent, high-ranking position indexed by significant wealth accumulation, leading economic competitiveness, strong diplomatic ties, stable government and English as lingua franca. What these translate into is a relatively more cushioned and carved out migration pathway in terms of visa application, skills recognition, employment opportunities, housing access and other settlement matters. Though my partner and I took about two years and several thousand dollars to eventually obtain our permanent residency offshore, our migration pathways were clearly mapped out by migration agents that we had the material resources to engage. Finally, I acknowledge that as a cisgender woman with straight passing privileges, I am spared from being violated, harassed, stared at and treated with hostility, which gender non-conforming and trans people are routinely forced to endure.

While I possess tremendous privileges as a Singaporean Chinese, middle-class, highly educated, English-speaking, able-bodied, cisgender woman in my home and host countries, I simultaneously encounter structural disadvantages at intersections of minoritization and marginalization. This indication is not meant to create victimhood and evoke sympathy. However, neither do I want to invalidate and downplay my racialized experiences and others in similar, diverse, multiple, overlapping, shifting and complicating encounters with dominant structures. As a racial minority subject in a white dominant society, an ethnic Chinese in the context of anti-Asian hate during the global pandemic and a queer woman in a heteronormative society, I have on more than one occasion experienced different, inter-related and perverse forms of racism, sexism, misogyny and queerphobia. But this is hardly the full story. The shock encounters with belittling, unbelonging and dehumanization are only the first part of the story. Unbeknownst to me earlier, the second part of the story involving punitive outcomes from protesting is the real hope-crashing devastation to an othered life. This book tells the second part of the story. It may likely strike a chord with readers who have undergone some form of similar gaslighting, silencing, erasure and punishment for speaking up and against dominance. Even if it does not, it hopes to invite readers to ask questions about taken for granted, interwoven structures of inequalities and injustices.

Back to the troubles …

I said at the beginning of the book that I got into serious trouble for complaining about racism. My hopelessly optimistic self with a deep belief in the goodness of humanity expected empathy and restorative justice. Not only did I not get the 'good triumphs evil' ending, but I also experienced close surveillance, gag orders and other punitive measures intended to keep me down and back in a subordinate place. To avoid further trouble and for the sake of self-preservation, no personal identifier and specifics of unfortunate incidents at the workplace will be included in this book. Having said that, I will, in this book, persist on naming and calling out systemic forces that exact violence against minoritized bodies.

It seems that my complaint and protest have probably threatened the oppressors' power and rattled them enough to launch an overzealous and extensive silencing campaign against me. By exposing and criticizing their colonial, racial capitalist, neoliberal and white supremacy projects and failing to be the compliant and complicit woman migrant subject they expected me to be, I was quickly singled out as the non-compliant troublemaker and harmony disrupter. White powers swiftly rained bureaucratic ammunitions that brought me to my knees and crushed my spirit. The brutal blows my racialized body came to bear resulted in a series of health issues including post-traumatic stress disorder, suicide ideation, self-harm, severe depression, severe anxiety and fibromyalgia flare-ups for most of 2020. It was also the year when the global Covid-19 pandemic brought the world to a halt and prevented me from visiting my home country and family. Strapped on board a prolonged emotional roller coaster in the middle of global and personal chaos, I ruminated and gaslit myself endlessly: Why did these troubles happen to me? Did I imagine them? Did I cause them? Was it my fault for stirring these troubles? Should I have just been a 'good Asian woman' and shut up?

In moments of self-blame, despair and injury, I turn to women of colour and Indigenous women feminist writings (see, for example, Davis 1983; Anzaldúa 1987; Lorde 1988; Moreton-Robinson 2020a; Mohanty 2003; hooks 2015; Ahmed 2017) for counsel, healing and rejuvenation. While these wonderful teachers provided therapy, clarity and purpose, an important validation came when I read the Women of Colour Australia 2021 survey findings. The survey reveals that women of colour in Australia experienced different forms of racism and xenophobia at the workplace, and their oppressions were exacerbated during the global Covid-19 pandemic (Women of Colour Australia 2021). The sample of over 500 survey respondents including 7 per cent who were Aboriginal and Torres Strait Islander across various industries and sectors related everyday experiences with racism in relation to language, accent, appearance, relationships with co-workers, group dynamics and performance expectations. To a certain extent, it is gratifying to see a survey like that receiving some media and scholarly attention. It piqued my curiosity about women of colour employees' experiences with racism and interrelated hegemonies at the workplace in the Australian academy. In an institution with an enterprise in increasing literacy and knowledge production, I wondered about its level of racial literacy and anti-racism commitments. These questions set me on a research journey to find answers.

Existing scholarly research has largely focused on gender discrimination against women at the workplace in Australia (see, for example, Gauci et al. 2022; Chang et al. 2014; Limpangog 2014; Hutchinson & Eveline 2010) including gender discrimination confronting women employees in the Australian academy (see, for example, Gilbert et al. 2021; Winchester & Browning 2015; Browning et al. 2013; Carrington & Pratt 2003). Though there is an existing field of study on racism confronting women of colour at the workplace in Australia (see, for example, Carangio et al. 2021; Nash & Moore 2020; Limpangog 2014), less attention has been given to women of colour employees in the Australian higher education sector and their encounters with intersectional hegemonies of racial capitalism, white supremacy and white patriarchy. Research on culturally and linguistically diverse women (CALD) employees' encounters with racism in Australian universities remains limited though I must acknowledge the valuable, brave and loud protests of Aboriginal women academics in Australian universities (see, for example, Moodie et al. 2022; Watego 2021; Moreton-Robinson 2020a).

A note on method

The book engages in storytelling to bear witness to Asian migrant women's stories. The Asian migrant woman is frequently racialized and feminized as a docile, obedient model migrant and (re)productive capitalist subject. Their cultural diversity is flattened by a common name, 'Asian', and with it comes expectations to be diligent, compliant and cooperative. While many suffer marginalization and debilitations from the violent workings of their host society's racial capitalist, neoliberal economy, they simultaneously labour hard for its prosperity, enjoy capital accumulation and earn their rightful place as the productive and successful migrant. Within this context of encountering colonization, racial capitalism and racism at the workplace, the book uncovers stories of the past and present to understand how ongoing effects of broader structural forces shape Asian diasporic women's migration trajectories, work experiences and everyday life. I turned to historical research studies that have excavated stories archives of early settler Asian migrant women in Singapore such as Chinese *Amah* and Indian *Ayah*. I dug through my own notes where I had earlier documented oral, autobiographical accounts my maternal grandmother, 婆婆 Popo, had related to me when she was alive. Over the years in the living room of her home, my late 婆婆 Popo had told me stories about her marriage migration from Palembang, Indonesia, to Singapore and subsequent work stints as a domestic servant and laundry lady in British colonial and Japanese expatriate households in 1950s and 1960s. Her stories are precious heirlooms she had gifted me. My 婆婆 Popo had seven children, and four of them were daughters. During the process of writing this book, I also consulted my mother and three maternal aunts about my grandmother's migration trajectories and domestic work experiences since my 婆婆 Popo had sadly passed on. They became important interlocutors of this study not only sharing family memories but also providing insights into local cultural references.

Connecting past trajectories to contemporary experiences of Asian migrant women, I tell my own stories as well as collect narratives of Asian women employees in Australian universities. Telling our stories here adds to the important archives of stories on Asian women's migration, displacement, racialization, privileges and feminisms. Together with the stories of the past and present, the book makes continuous and collective utterances about Asian migrant women's encounters with intersectional hegemonies. By offering my stories as part of research data, I make my experiences one of the sites of fieldwork research and knowledge production (Ellis & Bochner 2000; Ellingson 2006). I turn inward and embark on a self-scrutiny process to interrogate my privileges and complicity and reflect on the constraints and challenges I face in various contexts (Ellingson 2006). Subscribing to an anti-colonial feminist methodology, I take on a position that the researcher's experiences should not be exempt from research inquiry. It is therefore a deliberate methodological decision to include an autoethnographic approach and avail my personal experiences as one of the objects of analysis. In doing so, I aim to disrupt the unequal power relations between the researcher and the research subjects. Revealing my humanity, profanity, frailty and complexity, I seek to depart from the typically superior, detached, objective and aloof disposition of a researcher and shatter the barrier separating the researcher from their research subjects (Holman, Adams & Ellis 2013; Latham 2017).

I also listened deeply to forty Asian women employees working in Australian universities through one-on-one, in-depth interviews. The women responded to my advertised call for voluntary interview participants by contacting me and arranging for an online or in-person meeting. To carefully protect the women participants' anonymity and privacy, I have excluded their personal identifiers including name, nationality, cultural background, employer and area of work in direct quotes and only referred to them as 'respondents' in this book. The forty women I spoke with were either holding or have held a professional or academic position at different career stages and either on casual, permanent, part-time or full-time employment basis at an Australian university. They are from diverse nationality, ethnicity, age, gender, sexuality and ability backgrounds. They are first and second generation of immigrants from India, Bangladesh, Sri Lanka, Lebanon, Egypt, Iran, China, South Korea, Singapore, Malaysia, Vietnam, Thailand, Indonesia, The Philippines and reside across Australia including Western Australia, Victoria, South Australia and New South Wales. This qualitative data collection through in-depth interviews has undergone human research ethics approval and the forty respondents who volunteered to participate in this collective storytelling project have also been reimbursed with a modest gift voucher for their contributions to the project. I am profoundly privileged and honoured to listen to their open, honest and intimate stories on their own, as well as family migration experiences, and workplace encounters' with various forms of racialization, minoritization and marginalization. They also let me in to get a glimpse at their imaginations and hopes for more equitable and just futures and visions of collective solidarities.

A note on context

The book foregrounds Asian women employees' work experiences in Australian universities to explain the women's encounters with coloniality, white supremacy, racial capitalism and neoliberalism and reiterate the enduring reproduction of these violent forces in the institution of higher education. Why use the university as the study's object of analysis? I have been an Asian migrant woman employee of Australian universities and therefore am privy of the higher education sector's operation logics. I also have access to empirical data of Asian migrant women employees' lived work experiences in Australian universities since I am located within the institution. More importantly, there is an urgency to tell the stories of racialized, sexualized and othered bodies toiling at and for the epicentre of white supremacy and racial capitalism training. Speaking with the women and recollecting my own experiences, it raises more questions about the academy's role and responsibility in ensuring that the workplace for women of colour is culturally safe and allows them to survive, thrive and succeed. But many women I spoke with in this project were not surprised that their workplace in the Australian academy reeks of colonial and racial violence; one of them pointed out:

> This academy is a settler-colonial academy. We haven't come to terms with our history. The roots of settler-colonialism go very deep in this academy. This is a Eurocentric settler-colonial academy. Whose knowledge matters was decided a long time ago and then of course, neoliberalism just builds on that right? I mean, capitalism has always been racial right?

The modern university system that the world is familiar with has strong colonial roots where its original purpose of existence is to advance Western imperialism and liberalism (Hountondji 1997; Connell 2019). Paulin Hountondji (1997) in his anti-colonial work on African philosophy explains that colonizers extract knowledges, not just raw materials and minerals, from colonized Indigenous peoples, traffic the stolen knowledges to imperial centres, aggregate them in universities, libraries, museums and research institutes and transport it back to colonies and countries outside of the imperial centre as instructive and civilizing knowledges, concepts and methodologies. The Western university is a knowledge industrial system and 'key site through which colonialism – and colonial knowledge in particular – is produced, consecrated, institutionalised and naturalised' and where 'colonial intellectuals developed theories of racism, popularised discourses that bolstered support for colonial endeavours and provided ethical and intellectual grounds for the dispossession, oppression and domination of colonised subjects' (Bhambra, Gebrial & Nişancıoğlu 2018: 5). The Western university system is also brought to different parts of the world through colonialism and imperialism. Ma Rhea (1998) posits that the primary motivation and outcome of 'production and reproduction of ideas within the system of Commonwealth universities' is 'the globalisation of a scientific world view which is ontologically and epistemologically committed to the idea of "white superiority"' (Ma Rhea 1998: 3 as cited in Moreton-Robinson 2020a: 121–2). Contemporary universities around the world today model after the Western university and therefore continues to propagate the Western university's colonial legacy through formal education of Eurocentric ideals of civility, humanity, progress and freedom. The modern university and its curricula therefore continues to reinforce the global hierarchy of powers.

With its colonial and racial capitalist roots, it is unsurprising that the university responds and mutates in its extractive functions to align with the global neoliberal economy. Scholars (Mbembe 2016; Connell 2019) have observed that universities around the world are increasingly aligned with profit-driven and corporate managerial modus. Universities appear to take the corporate sector's lead in organization management and discourse shifts. In the area of employee management, some of the noticeable moves include changing the department's name of human resource to people and culture and shifting the focus from affirmative actions and equal opportunity to equity, diversity and inclusion (EDI). Often these corporate managerial changes mirror the profit sector and take on an economically rational and neoliberal logic to maximize capital and improve business performance through optimization (or some would argue, exploitation) of human resources (Mbembe 2016; Connell 2019). Achille Joseph Mbembe (2016) laments that 'universities today are large systems of authoritative control, standardisation, gradation, accountancy, classification, credits and penalties … and they have turned higher education into a marketable product, rated, bought and sold by standard units, measured, counted and reduced to staple equivalence by impersonal, mechanical tests and therefore readily subject to statistical consistency, with numerical standards and units' (2016: 30). There is expectedly a lesser or no focus on social justice principles and anti-colonial and intersectional feminist philosophies in the increasingly corporatized university.

From Rhodes Must Fall at University of Cape Town, South Africa (Kamanzi 2015), to Why is My Curriculum White? at University College London (Tehrani 2015), there have been movements to interrogate the colonial roots of contemporary universities at the metropole and in former colonies, challenge the naturalness, neutrality and dominance of colonial knowledges in existing curricula and universities and expose ongoing perpetuation of coloniality and racism through the global Western university system. The collision of coloniality and anti-coloniality cannot be more pronounced at the university where colonial knowledges are continually produced and the calls to decolonize knowledge, curriculum and the university are getting louder around the world. However, even well-meaning universities who seek to 'decolonize' their curriculum struggle to break free of Euro-US-centric benchmarks of what counts as knowledge and science. Strong rebuttals of empty, tokenistic 'decolonizing', 'indigenizing' and 'diversifying' smokescreens that only treat decolonization as a metaphor and reinforce status quo of white dominance could also be heard (Tuck & Yang 2012; Bhambra, Gebrial & Nişancıoğlu 2018). Located at such a unique workplace that continues to be instrumental in reproducing coloniality, Western imperialism, racial capitalism, neoliberalism and global inequalities, the stories of Asian migrant women employees in Australian universities need to be told. Their stories revealing how they contribute to, are complicit in, benefit from as well as suffer from the higher education industrial complex in Australian settler-colonial society need to be heard.

In my earlier work (Quah 2021), I have argued for the importance of employing anti-coloniality and social justice principles to improve work environments of women academics located at the intersections of multiple oppressions such as racism, sexism and ableism. In the context of challenging racism and other intersectional hegemonies in universities, I advocate for resisting the increasing corporatization of universities' modus operandi and bringing the discourse on employees' workplace health and safety, employment satisfaction and career development back to the social justice, anti-coloniality, anti-racism and anti-neoliberalism framework. But before all these could be materialized, the academy must confront its colonial legacies, racial capitalist roots and neoliberal inclinations. If the university's original mission is to educate and produce knowledge so as to better the society, would it not be necessary for the university to reflect upon its mandate and consider how it treats its students and employees, in particular women of colour employees located at the intersection of multiple structural challenges? In that context, this book is also interested to explore if universities' EDI efforts to 'empower' women and promote equitable access and participation are truly effective in addressing systemic issues, particularly racism that debilitates women of colour employees in Australian universities. Or are they just a smokescreen for universities to engage in whitewashing and pinkwashing trickery to deflect attention from their racial capitalist aggressions in advancing and maintaining white dominance? By excavating Asian migrant women employees' stories and investigating into Australian universities' public mandates and efforts on EDI and the likes, the book seeks to find some answers to these questions.

Fire Dragon Feminism hopes to offer an anti-colonial, anti-racial capitalism feminist framework for Asian migrant woman subjects in the contexts of global neoliberal economy and Asia-Pacific settler and postcolonial societies. While there has been an extensive body of literature on racialization of Asian Americans and the notion of Asian model minority in American capitalist society (just to name a few: Trinh T.Minh-ha (1989) *Woman, native, other*; Rosalind S. Chou and Joe R. Feagin (2015) *The myth of the model minority*; Anne Anlin Cheng's (2019) *Ornamentalism*; Cathy Park Hong (2020) *Minor feelings: A reckoning on race and the Asian condition*), there is significant potential for consolidation of research and writings on Asian migrant women in other parts of the world, specifically, Asia-Pacific settler and postcolonial societies. The book is an anti-colonial effort to decentre feminist strands emerging out of the Global North, that is United States and Western Europe. Arguably, women of colour feminist strands, such as Black, Latina, Asian American and Chicana feminisms emerging from America and Europe continents, do not speak to the specificities of the Asia-Pacific settler and postcolonial histories and contexts and the Asian woman migrant capitalist subjects navigating their migrant existence in these societies. A feminist framework is therefore needed for Asian woman migrant subjects in Asia-Pacific settler and postcolonial societies. The book offers a migrant feminist framework for Asian migrant woman subjects to account for their shifting migrant position, capital accumulation, complicities, racialization, responsibilities and activisms. I do so by advancing fire dragon feminism as a migrant feminist framework and hope it will contribute to global feminist, race and migration scholarship on migrant women of colour's encounters with colonization, racial capitalism and neoliberalism.

Book structure

In the next chapter, I dive into the conceptual framework of *Fire Dragon Feminism*. The chapter provides insights into the histories, epistemes, ontologies and methodologies that shape fire dragon feminism framework. I express my anxieties about self-exoticizing and self-orientalizing with the reference of Chinese mythical creature, fire dragon and caution readers against constructing tokenistic 'authentic', exotic cultural pride stories in the name of 'decolonization' which would only backfire and end up satisfying the Western gaze once again. In full acknowledgement of the risks of conjuring racialized, orientalized stereotypes of Asiatic femininity, I handle carefully the mythology of fire dragon from Dragon Princess or Dragon Daughter in Buddhist sutras to Little Dragon Maiden in Chinese literatures to contemporary derogatory cultural references of Little Dragon Woman. I explain that the aim of evoking Chinese mythology of fire dragon is not to re-orientalize Asian women and reinforce Western imperial frames of racializing and othering Asian women but rather to confront head-on the myths, good and bad, imposed on Asian migrant women subjects. To unpack these racialized and sexualized myths of Asian migrant women, it is important to account for the historical contexts and colonial legacies Asian migrant women have come to inherit and continue to be affected by persistent racialized power structures. The chapter excavates historical research to consider the migration trajectories of early settler Asian migrant women in Asia-Pacific region, including *Amah* and *Ayah* (domestic servants from East and South Asia) and my maternal grandmother, who moved to Singapore as an accompanying wife from Palembang, Indonesia, worked as a domestic servant in British colonial and Japanese expatriate households in Singapore. I set out to explain the historical context of early Asian migrant women's participations, implications, complicity, racialization and sexualization in colonial projects. I discuss how colonial histories lay the foundation of today's global extraction of resources, hierarchy of nations and uneven distribution of life chances, and account for the interconnected contexts of racialization of Asian migrant women during the colonial period, the colonial legacy of racialization and sexualization contemporary Asian migrant women have come to inherit and the continuous racialization and sexualization they are subjected to in present neoliberal projects. I show how the emergence of rising Asian economies sees to Asian migrant women's capital accumulation as well as encounters with racial violence and xenophobia. Narrowing to the specific context of Asian migrant women in white settler colonial Australian society, the chapter goes on to explain how early Asian immigrant women like Chinese *Amahs*, Indian *Ayahs* and accompanying wives were directly implicated in settler-colonialism projects dispossessing Indigenous peoples, grabbing lands and plundering resources when they supplied domestic and intimate labour in the reproduction of settler households. In contemporary Australian points-based immigration application system, the productive value and potential attached to Asian immigrant women, while elevates their socio-economic positions in Australian society, also reinforces their racialization as model minority and desirable citizen. I show how the Asian migrant woman subject is once again assigned to the aesthetic, ornamental and supplementary role in Australian nation-building, white race-making project. This project uses the particular case study of Asian migrant women employees in the Australian academy to explain the women's encounters with coloniality, white supremacy, racial capitalism and neoliberalism and reiterate the enduring reproduction of such violent structures in the institution of higher education. I clarify the purpose of fire dragon feminism as one that examines migrant women's implications, privileges and complicity in global colonial and neoliberal projects, as well as their responsibilities and strategies in denouncing extractive and exploitative forces, reorganizing rules and building solidarity for more sustainable and just futures.

Chapter 3 returns to my troubles and connects them to stories shared generously by forty Asian migrant women employees of Australian universities. The forty women and I came together to speak against the myths that have been imposed on us, speak about the injuries inflicted as a result and speak up about the ways we attempt to break free of the constrictions. Our stories hope to open up an investigation and contribute a way of thinking, interpreting and recording of Asian migrant women's racialized experiences in Australian academy and wider settler-colonial Australian society. Our stories join long-established, collective utterances and protests by race-critical, feminist and queer scholar-activists against oppressive structures that are always already set out to dominate and subjugate non-white subjects in the white, colonial academy. The chapter organizes the women's stories in three sections to discuss racialized myths they must deal with at the workplace. By exposing these myths, it is not to argue for the women's visibility and recognition since such debates often degenerate into a portrayal of victimhood and knee-jerk activation of white benevolent rescue missions. It is also not to whine about how Asian migrant women have been neglected, forgotten and left in the corner while white powers give other minoritized groups attention. Falling into the trappings of Oppression Olympics (Hancock 2011) to fight to be 'included' and receive whatever crumbs minoritized subjects are allowed to have are certainly not the outcomes the project seeks. Rather, I am interested to use historicized and anti-colonial perspectives to understand how Asian migrant women are set up to encounter certain racialized myths, how their realities are affected by these myths and how such myths are often far from truths. The myth of being seen as non-white, non-Indigenous, not racialized subjects has a colonial context to it. I discuss how the colonial division of labour set Asian immigrant women up to occupy a transient, ornamental, supplementary and intermediary role in colonial, white race-making projects. It may appear Asian migrant women subjects are not white, Black and racialized, but the colonial division of labour has indeed subject them to a racialized role supporting the reproduction of white heteropatriarchal institutions. The women's narratives present sufficient evidence of how they have been racialized, sexualized and ornamentalized in the classroom, research space and university's administrative functions, and how their exoticization and infantilization conscript and implicate them in white race-making in the academy. Another racialized myth the women's stories reveal is the myth of being a well-poised, mobile and achieving migrant woman. What living with this imposed myth often means that the women engaged in self-surveillance, self-censorship and self-capacitation to fulfil imposed racialized myths and roles and be white enough for white people to interact with them albeit condescendingly. Their stories show that they were not exactly autonomous and mobile Asian migrant women employees with equitable access to physical, social and professional spaces. Sometimes through hard lessons, they learned about the perimeters of enclosure they were permitted to move within and the manner and pace they must move in to avoid rousing white rage, insecurity and disapproval. In addition, since Asian migrant women in the university are commonly perceived as well-adjusted, ambitious, successful and composed professionals, their racialization and racial injuries were not always apparent in popular imagination of racism and minoritization. The women in this study, however, reported extensive costs of racism to their safety, livelihood, work life, career progression, financial status, access to permanent housing and home ownership, social relationships, physical and mental health and wellbeing and aspirations. The third myth that this chapter deals with is the myth of minoritized communities being homogenous and safe. There is a common assumption and expectation that minoritized subjects bound by marginalizations, albeit difference in intersectional forms and manifestations, would stand in solidarity with one another. However, the women's stories expose lateral violence from fellow people of colour co-workers and students who have learnt the oppressor's ways and wield the oppressor's weapons against them. Rather than focusing on marginalized subjects' internalized racism and remedial actions to correct internalized racism and self-fulfilling prophetical behaviours, I am more interested in moving away from an individualistic approach to discuss how certain structural conditions promote violence laterally, horizontally among oppressed minoritized populations. My discussion here highlights how the settler-colonial system introduced a racial hierarchy that not only placed white European Anglo-Saxon populations at the top rung but also stratified minoritized populations according to colonialists' arbitrary definition and ranking of humanity. The racial hierarchal system therefore already set colonizied Indigenous peoples and minoritized non-white subjects to compete against each other and among themselves for resources. What is also important to note is minoritized subjects' proximity to white settler-colonial racial capitalist projects and how that in turn brings about heterogenous and shifting responses to racialized environments, and at times, compelling some to disassociate, assimilate and display white majority's ways for survival, safety, stability and capacitation. Paying close attention to the women's stories, the chapter shows how the specificities and hybridities of their migration histories, trajectories and circumstances interact with colonialism, racial capitalism and neoliberalism in the university.

Chapter 4 goes on to discuss a specific manifestation of racial capitalism and neoliberalism in the academy – the Equity, Diversity and Inclusion programme and Asian migrant women employees' encounters with their workplace's EDI initiatives. Using the same framework of exposing myths and accounting Asian migrant women employees' experiences with such myths, the chapter deals with four specific myths observed in the women's narratives. The four myths the chapter seeks to expose include the myth of essentialized and compartmentalized selves in identity-focused EDI; myth of 'intersectionality'; myth of 'diversity, inclusion and harmony'; and myth of 'individual responsibility and allyship'. A prominent myth in existing corporatized EDI programme is the neat compartmentalization of identity-based diversity work. The main problem of corporatized, compartmentalized identity-focused EDI lies with essentializing, disintegrating and compartmentalizing one's multiple selves and expecting one to perform and conform to constructed myths of each identity category. The chapter turns to the women's stories and reveals how they are often pigeonholed to perform specific identity-based diversity work and must do so within defined perimeters and expectations of power holders to avoid retribution and repercussions. Their narratives also show how the preoccupation with identity classification, representation and struggles in identity-driven EDI programmes dehistorizes, decontexualizes and manages differences based on the institution's definitions of gender, sexuality and cultural identities and thresholds for differences. I turn to Paul Preciado's (2020) position on disidentification and anti-identity politics to consider how we may transform and reorganize the corporate EDI space into a collective solidarity platform for social justice and sustainability. Unfortunately, in response to critiques of diversity and inclusion programmes as being singularly focused on particular individual social identities in separate, compartmentalized focus areas, the buzzword of 'intersectionality' is often thrown in the mix to appease critics and minorities who feel that their needs and concerns have not been meaningfully recognized and addressed. Joining critics of appropriation and corporatization of intersectionality, I show how an additive 'intersectional' approach driven by identity and representation politics does not dismantle unequal power structures but instead conceals subjects' political relationality and embeddedness in unequal power structures and upholds the interests of white supremacy, colonialism and racial capitalism. I suggest countering depoliticized, identitarian intersectionality with relational intersectionality exposing unequal power relations constitutive of colonial histories and contemporary racial capitalist political and economic contexts and making dominant white powers visible and accountable. The corporate EDI programme is also particularly obsessed with 'inclusion and harmony' eager to present a harmonious picture of empowered minorities of diverse backgrounds. Shiny corporate posters splashed across billboards and social media feeds featuring staff and students of as many diverse demographic characteristics as possible only create the myth that we have come a long way and progressed to a more equitable and just place for minorities. This corporate branding exercise arguably helps power holders sleep better and blunts consciousness of subordinated peoples. The women's narratives also show how those who told the truths about colonialism, racial capitalism, white supremacy and privilege inevitably faced punishment for disrupting the harmony orchestrated by dominant powers. When they turned to the university's complaint mechanism to lodge their own complaints against racism and related discriminatory treatments, they soon found out that the official complaint mechanism was not meant for minoritized staff members to protest against institutional racism and seek redress. In the final section of this chapter, I unpack the myth of individual responsibility and allyship across the full suite of EDI programmes including anti-racism, cultural safety, prevention of sexual harassment and sexual assault, LGBTIQA+ support and staff health and well-being. I demonstrate how the business model is driven by an individualist, self-responsibilizing approach where the ownership to manage risk of violence and create a harmonious and safe work environment lies with individual staff members. I argue that no matter how well-meaning and sincere these individual-focused EDI efforts are, historical, inherited and interrelated asymmetrical power relations and structures are left uninterrogated. Instead of attacking dominant power structures that result in the contemporary problems of inequalities, violence and injustices the world is plagued with, the existing approach only seems to make us busy with individual identity markers, inclusion efforts, diversity celebrations and ally training programmes that do nothing to dismantle unjust hierarchal structures, reorganize relations and improve equitable access to life chances and safety. I emphasize that my critiques of corporate EDI programmes stem from an opposition of white supremacy, racial capitalism and neoliberalism.

The final chapter of the book presents the hopes of the study's women respondents – their hopes of breaking free of racialization and ornamentalism, being supported by and colluding with people who get race, and having an anti-colonialism, anti-racism, anti-racial capitalism and anti-neoliberalism workplace and academy. In response to Saidiya Hartman's (2022) reflection on the coloniality of explanations and call to be 'freer and freer' in presenting narratives, the concluding chapter features poems by selected Asian migrant women scholars and activists inviting us to glimpse into snippets of their experiences of migration, racism and womanhood. I end the book paying tribute and celebrating grassroots feminist activisms that are agitating, abolishing and reorganizing existing colonial, racial capitalist and neoliberal structures deeply embedded in the academy and different facets of the global society. The conclusion features Intan Paramaditha, Indonesian of Sumatran-Sundanese heritage, anti-colonial feminist academic and writer; Israa Merhi, a second-generation descendant of Lebanese Muslim immigrant family, poet and activist for Indigenous land rights; Sukhmani Khorana of Sikh-Indian heritage, academic, author and advocate for migrants and refugees in the Global North; Helena Liu, intersectional feminist academic and activist of Chinese-Fuzhou heritage; Souheir Edelbi, a second-generation descendant of Lebanese immigrant family in Australia, who researches and teaches on race-making, coloniality and international justice, specifically, Palestinian liberation. The book is ultimately a loud proclamation of the women's refusal to settle for a quiet, corporative, good migrant woman existence co-opted by the extractive cooperate machinery. By telling our stories (you can never tell them enough!), we stand alongside other women of colour who have struggled with, staged refusal and blown flames at colonization, racial capitalism and neoliberalism. The book ends with a reminder that fire dragon feminism is an ongoing, life-long, never complete migrant feminist activism that exposes racialized myths imposed on minoritized migrant subjects and archives and activates anti-coloniality, anti-racial capitalism abolitionist and reorganizing strategies.

2

Fire dragon feminism

I am anxious about self-racialization …

By turning to Chinese mythology of fire dragon, I am anxious about exoticizing my cultural heritage and, as a result, end up re-orientalizing and self-racializing and consequently reproduce the very colonial, imperial and Orientalist frames that I have been critiquing and resisting. I am mindful of such common traps of 'decolonizing' efforts where even well-intentioned anti-colonial scholars, grassroots activists and community workers find themselves caught up with unknowingly. Often, out of an impulse to retaliate against Euro-American imperialism and everyday institutional and casual racisms, these actors, in the name of 'decolonization', turn to mythologizing 'cultural and native roots' and creating seemingly 'authentic' cultural narratives (Quah & Tang 2024). To be clear, there is certainly tremendous value in excavating and revitalizing cultures and languages that were erased and suppressed during colonial times. However, it is a delicate balance to maintain. It is one thing to reclaim cultural practices, traditional beliefs and languages that were branded as uncivilized and disallowed to exist by colonial powers. It is another thing to create cultural myths reproducing orientalism and self-racialization for the sake of differentiating non-Western cultures from dominant West. These well-meaning 'non-West versus the West' cultural projects while on the one hand enhance racial-national and ethno-cultural pride, on the other, re-orientalize non-Western cultures as exotic objects to be studied by the Western gaze and even commodified and profited for the global market's consumption of their 'authenticity and exoticism'. This is what Ari Larissa Heinrich (2013) has argued earlier that such 'decolonizing', 'us versus the West' efforts would only strengthen the colonial, imperial and Orientalist frames that the anti-colonial actors seek to resist and critique. I am therefore anxious that my foregrounding of Chinese mythology of fire dragon and conceptualization of fire dragon feminism will not fall into the same trappings of mythologizing Asian, Southeast Asian and Chinese cultural heritage and constructing tokenistic 'authentic', exotic cultural pride stories. I am well aware that if the latter happens, I will only satisfy Western imperial appetites for native exoticism, please civil liberals and liberal feminists for 'returning to and being proud of my roots' and whitewash unequal power structures by fitting into institution-prescribed cultural diversity boxes.

By writing about fire dragon feminist and Asian migrant women, I am cognizant of the risk of conjuring the all too familiar ornamental personhood the yellow woman has historically and persistently through contemporary times been implicated in the making of Western modern personhood (Cheng 2019). The yellow woman, as Anne Anlin Cheng (2019) observes, is 'encrusted by representations, abstracted and reified', 'persistently sexualised yet barred from sexuality, simultaneously made and unmade by the aesthetic project' and 'like the proverbial Ming vase, … at once ethereal and base'. Cheng (2019) indicates that the yellow woman in her Asiatic femininity, decorative purpose 'prosthetic humanness', 'aesthetic being' and ornamental personhood speaks to the well-documented, long-standing racializing, sexualizing, objectifying and dehumanizing of Asian women (2019: 16). The latter have been delegated to the category of aesthetic non-living living thing in the making of modern Euro-American masculine personhood (Cheng 2019: 22). I am concerned that references to fire dragon feminism may reinforce long-standing stereotypes of Asiatic femininity as Oriental exotic, ornamental extravagant like the Hollywood's fantasies of Dragon Lady, Japanese geisha and Chinese concubine (Prasso 2005) and consequently contribute to the construction of Western modern personhood with their accessorising, aesthetic ornamental presence. With these knowledges and anxieties, I tread carefully as I consider the mythology of fire dragon and conceptualization of fire dragon feminism.

Fire dragon: Parallels between myths and realities

Asian migrant women have been associated and perplexed with multiple imageries of inspiring and as well as, disparaging meanings unfortunately. The term 'dragon lady' has commonly been associated with portrayal of Asian women in popular Hollywood movies as scheming and ruthless (Shah 1997; Prasso 2005) and even landed with a definition of 'an overbearing and tyrannical woman' in the 1996 *Meriam-Webster's dictionary* (Shah 1997: xiv). Contributing to the overall Orientalist discourse of Yellow Peril in European, Northern American and Australian settler-colonial societies as early as 1800s lasting till today with recent Covid-19 pandemic-related anti-Asian racism in 2020–2, Dragon Lady symbolizing Asian migrant women has been described as yet another evil from the East responsible for contaminating their good white society. It is however important to note that 'Dragon Lady' bears different meanings and symbolic purposes for different people and communities beyond being the dominant derogatory symbol of Oriental debauchery.

For example, 龙女, directly translated as Dragon Woman or Dragon Lady, features significantly in a major branch of Buddhism, Mahayana Buddhism. In Lotus Sutra, a key scripture of Mahayana Buddhism, its Devadatta chapter or chapter 12 describes 龙女 as an extraordinary eight-year-old daughter of the dragon king (Abé 2015) and references 龙女 as Dragon Princess or Dragon Daughter though the term directly translates to Dragon Woman or Dragon Lady. The Lotus Sutra records that 龙女, Dragon Princess or Dragon Daughter, attained enlightenment after presenting a legendary pearl to Buddha on behalf of her dragon king father (see Figure 2.1). She is celebrated for her extraordinary

Figure 2.1 Sutra art from the Heike-Nôkyô; the mikaeshi of chapter 12, Lotus Sutra.

wisdom and enlightenment in arriving Buddhahood or Bodhi at such a young age. It is interesting to note that the Lotus Sutra also records the strong objections 龙女 faced in her attempt to attain Buddhahood. Her opposers argued that 'a woman's body is soiled and thus cannot serve as a vessel to advance the Mahayana', and a woman herself would also face '五障 five obstructions' to achieve enlightenment (Abé 2015: 36). The scriptures, however, write that Buddha intervenes and affirms 龙女's attainment. Her story becomes a reminder that women can become buddhas too. While the scriptures indicate that Buddha objected to patriarchal notions where women's bodies are tainted and could not attain Buddhahood and proceeded to give 龙女 a seal of approval, the parable in the end reconciles with patriarchal values by including an important detail that 龙女 rebirthed as a man to achieve the highest level of Buddhahood (Abé 2015). The message here is that women can become buddha but in order to reach a level comparable with Buddha, they need to become a man first. This is a profound yet typical discovery on 龙女's myths. The legend relates women's entanglements with constrictive obstacles patriarchy presents, their attempts to break free of such chokeholds and somehow inescapable conformity with men's rules to achieve the highest form of success.

Transnational flow of Buddhism, Buddhist scriptures and Indian Buddhist literatures from India to China brought about proliferation of Indian-Chinese folklores and literary works on the dragon king and dragon girl or daughter or princess. What followed was the metamorphosis of Indian Buddhist's Dragon Lady into a wide variety of Chinese literary works dated as early as Six Dynasties (AD 220–589) and reaching its peak in Tang Dynasty (AD 618–690; 705–907) (Zheng 1997). This body of Chinese literatures took on the Lotus Sutra's characterization of 龙女 Dragon Lady as a woman warrior of extraordinary bravery, wisdom and divine power and fused it with local historical, cultural and social contexts and folklores to produce many more adaptations (Zheng 1997). What is interesting to note is that the interactions between Indian-Buddhism and Chinese societies inspired the embodiment of transnational and intercultural interactions in the development of mixed-race Dragon Lady characterization in Chinese literary works during these periods of Chinese dynasties (Zheng 1997).

Remarkably, Chinese societies' fascination with Dragon Lady endures through centuries and continues to populate print and screen media in contemporary times. In particular, a Chinese martial arts novel, 神雕俠侶 *The return of the condor heroes*, published in 1959 by well-known People's Republic of China (PRC)-born, Hong Kong-based writer 金庸 Jin Yong features a prominent fictional character 小龙女 Little Dragon Maiden (see Figure 2.2) and has been adapted into multiple popular drama series over several decades in Hong Kong, PRC and Singapore. In this widely known story across Chinese societies, 小龙女 is an esteemed, highly skilled martial arts warrior. At the age of fourteen, she assumed leadership of the martial arts sect who adopted her when she was abandoned on the street at birth. She was named 小龙女 after the Chinese zodiac year of dragon she was born in. Here again, Dragon Lady is portrayed as an extraordinary woman warrior who displays exceptional talents and leadership qualities at a young age, akin to the dragon maiden mentioned in the Lotus Sutra. What is noteworthy in this popular novel is that the author, 金庸 Jin Yong, chose to centre 小龙女, his lead woman character's romantic

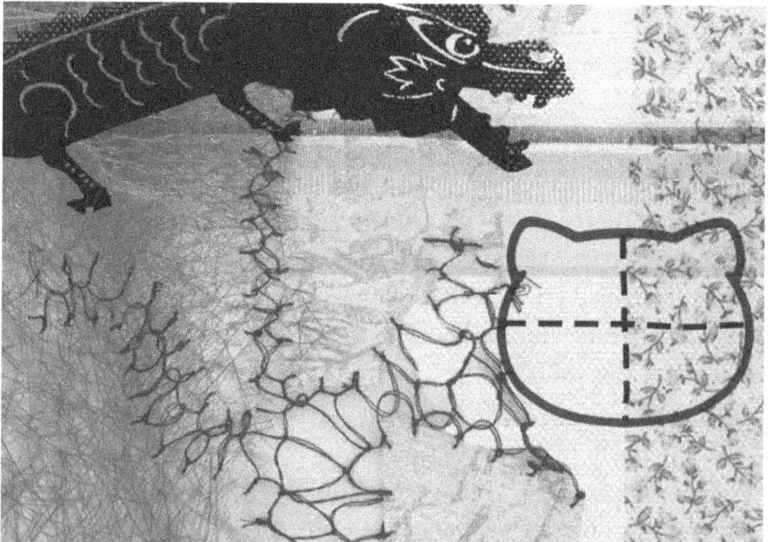

Figure 2.2 Artistic visualization of Fire Dragon Feminism by visual artist, Yanti Peng, a Metal Dragon Chinese first-generation immigrant in Australia.

relationship with her younger male disciple. Not only is the master-disciple romance a taboo in the martial arts community during the period the novel is set in, but also the feature of intimate relationship between an older woman and a younger man would have also been trailblazing in Chinese societies at the time the story was written and published. Both characterizations of 龙女 Dragon Lady in the early Indian Buddhist scriptures and contemporary Chinese literary works call attention to the women's queering of dominant standards imposed on women in specific contexts they are located in and their extraordinary feats in breaking free of constrictive patriarchal and heteronormative structures. Both Dragon Lady legends leave behind deep cultural imprints of feminine attributes and woman warriorship in popular imaginations across Asian societies. However, at the same time, both dragon women stories sharply reveal the ways in which deeply entrenched systems of patriarchy, sexism and misogyny control and restrict women in their respective contexts and times.

For the past two decades, the image of Dragon Lady has unfortunately come to bear deprecating connotations. In early 2000s, derogatory cultural references of 小龙女 Little Dragon Woman emerged in Southeast Asian societies such as Singapore, Malaysia and Thailand. The negative label was given to PRC-born women sex workers engaged in illegal sex work at nightclubs, karaoke bars and brothels (Meng & Chen 2006). Other disparaging terms such as 乌鸦 Crow (BBC Chinese 2001); China Girl (Henson 2004); 中国妹 China Sister (Meng & Chen 2006); and 中国娃娃 China Doll (Shi 2010) were also added to the anti-PRC Chinese women racist lexicon in these Southeast Asian-ethnic Chinese societies. These names carry a persistent xenophobic, racist and sexist subtext that PRC-born women are money-grabbing and have infiltrated Southeast Asian societies to extract money from local men, wreck families and create havoc in otherwise peaceful and stable societies. Widespread inflammatory accounts on how PRC-born Chinese immigrant women destroy marriages by being a mistress or '第三者 the third party' in extramarital affairs; work illegally as sex workers and get rounded up in police raids at bars and nightclubs; enter sham marriages for permanent residency and citizenship and cheat their citizen husband of money before dumping them for another man; find themselves a sugar daddy or work as an escort while on a student's visa; and seek work as a masseur that provides additional sex service for extra cash while being on a student guardian or long-term social visit visa as a 陪读妈妈 study mother or parental guardian for their school-going child circulate widely in mainstream and social media (for example, BBC Chinese 2001; Henson 2004; Meng & Chen 2006; Chan 2011). My 姨姨 youngest maternal aunty, one of the important interlocuters of this study, has gathered decades of stories and insights from her workplace as a retail assistant, patronage at local bars and '咖啡店 kopitiams' (colloquial term in Hokkien dialect for local coffee shops in Singapore) and consumption of everyday mainstream and tabloid news. She related this when I asked her about the cultural reference of 小龙女:

> At one point many China women came to Singapore. Some are study mothers. Some are from unknown backgrounds. They used to operate from Chinatown and some hung around the rooftop garden of People's Park market. They seduced old married Singaporean Chinese men and disappeared after cheating them of money. These old men after being cheated, lost their wife and children and ended up homeless and stranded on the streets. They sought help from the government but there were too many cases like that. In the end the government changed the law where the retirement funds' withdrawal age became 65 years old instead of the original 55 years old, and limited the withdrawal amount where retirees could only have an instalment amount each month instead of withdrawing all of it and squandering or getting cheated by these women. This in the end caused so much troubles and harmed local Singaporean women.

Interestingly, the local sentiments revealed resentment towards Chinese foreign women and saw them as threats and ills, while local citizen men came out blameless and seen as the innocent, gullible victims.

Such xenophobic sentiments about Asian foreign women and marriage migrant women extend beyond PRC Chinese women to other migrant women from less wealthy countries in the region such as Malaysia, Vietnam, Cambodia and Thailand. The prejudiced discourse against lower-income Asian migrant women is certainly not unique in Singaporean society but also in other wealthier migrant-receiving countries. In my previous study on marriage migrant women, transnational families and divorce (Quah 2020a), I have also shown how such racist and xenophobic notions about foreign women from less wealthy countries out to cheat, plunder and extract resources from hardworking, unsuspecting men and families of their wealthier host society seep right into seemingly neutral and rational official immigration and family policies to 'protect' local populations and safeguard national resources. Specific marriage, family, immigration and retirement funds policies have been developed and implemented based largely on nationalistic, xenophobic and paternalistic beliefs that good, honest local citizen men must be protected from foreign, conniving women from less wealthy countries. It is not hard to observe that seditious portrayals in both popular and official discourses impact the migration experience of Chinese immigrant women where blows of xenophobia and racism hurled against them in insidious and overt ways affect every aspect of their settlement including employability, work, housing access, living conditions and social relationships. Some nightlife businesses even went to the extent of putting up signs at the entrance and disallowing Chinese women from entering and patronizing their establishments out of fear of attracting potential reports of illicit sex activities and subsequent police raids (Meng & Chen 2006). Extensive scholarly research studies have also discussed the unfavourable dimensions of migration and settlement experiences of PRC-born Chinese immigrant women across Asian societies, for example challenges faced by Chinese study mothers in Singapore (Huang & Yeoh 2005; Yeoh & Huang 2010; gendered racialization of new Chinese migrant women in Singapore (Ang 2016, 2021, 2022); othering of Chinese migrant women in Malaysia (Yoong & Lee 2023); and more generally, discrimination against and impact on Chinese migrant women in Southeast Asia (Shi 2010).

Part of this assemblage of myths on Dragon Lady is the Chinese mythology of fire dragon. The symbol of fire dragon carries a highly auspicious connotation. In Asian societies, especially ethnic Chinese communities, fire dragon bears significant symbolic meanings of majestic powers, supernatural might and heavenly greatness. There are twelve zodiac animal signs in 十二生肖 Chinese horoscope – 鼠 rat, 牛 ox, 虎 tiger, 兔 rabbit, 龙 dragon, 蛇 snake, 马 horse, 羊 goat, 猴 monkey, 鸡 rooster, 狗dog and 猪 pig. There are five elements, 五行 in Chinese zodiac. The five elements 五行 are 金 Metal, 木 Wood, 水 Water, 火 Fire and 土 Earth. In Chinese mythology, the dragon has been referred to as the god of clouds and rain and the king of seas. The symbol of dragon was reserved for Chinese emperors of multiple late Chinese dynasties, hence further elevating its sacred and royal image. I grew up watching Chinese period dramas that featured Chinese emperors wearing golden robes embroidered with dragons and anyone who used or wore the dragon symbol would be charged of treason and face execution by beheading. There is also a folklore that Chinese populations are 龙的传人, the descendants of dragon, which reveals a strong sense of cultural pride and superiority. Chinese parents, commonly 望子成龙, hope that their child will one day become a dragon, which does signify not only achievement of success but also attainment of true destiny.

Against this cultural backdrop, it is no surprise that baby booms could be observed in dragon years across Chinese societies in China, Hong Kong, Taiwan, Singapore and Malaysia (Goodkind 1991). For example, in Singapore, it has been reported that fertility rates in dragon years are higher than in other years, especially the tiger years where Chinese couples avoid childbirth (Tan 2023). According to official statistics, the total fertility rate for Singaporean-Chinese population dipped to 0.87 in the Year of Tiger in 2022, as compared to 1.18 in the Year of Dragon in 2012 (Tan 2023). The combination of Chinese zodiac sign of dragon and the element of fire is believed to ordain one with the most auspicious, prosperous, successful and formidable destiny. This combination is therefore arguably to be the most desired zodiac. Understandably, there was a baby boom in 1976, the Year of Fire Dragon across ethnic Chinese communities including Singapore, Malaysia and Taiwan (Tan 2023). What that also means is that Fire Dragon 1976 babies in countries with significant ethnic Chinese populations arguably face heightened competition for access to resources and opportunities in education, employment and housing. Born in 1976, I am one of these 火龙 fire dragon babies growing up with a larger birth cohort in an already intensely competitive Singaporean society. Not only do fire dragon babies in Chinese societies live under the expectations that fire dragon babies are destined to do great things and yield extraordinary success according to Chinese mythology, but many also live with relatively greater stress in competing for resources to survive and thrive having born in a larger birth cohort. Researchers have shown that larger birth cohorts suffer worse life prospects and outcomes due to increased competition (Tan 2023). For example, in Singapore, 'Singaporean Chinese born in the Year of the Dragon earn lower income than other Chinese birth cohorts' and even other population groups not born in the Year of Dragon who enter the workforce as dragon cohorts consequently face greater competition and more stressful employment, wage and overall life prospects (Tan 2023). One can imagine how these population groups' life chances will be further challenged if they also face marginalization by intersectional dominant systems of race, heteronormativity, patriarchy and body ableism. Ironically, it turns out that Chinese parents, who have chosen to give birth to dragon babies in hope of giving their child a head start in life with an auspicious astronomical destiny, end up setting their dragon child up on a more treacherous path competing for limited opportunities and successes with a larger birth cohort.

The aim of evoking Chinese mythology of fire dragon or Dragon Lady is not to re-orientalize Asian women and reinforce Western imperial frames of racializing and othering Asian women. Rather, fire dragon feminism is about confronting head-on all of these myths, whether they are inspirational references of extraordinary aptitudes like 龙女 in Buddhism's Lotus Sutra, 小龙女 in Chinese literary works, 火龙 fire dragon in Chinese astrology or demeaning constructs reflecting xenophobia, racism, Sinophobia and sexism. The framework seeks to understand how Asian migrant women's lives are shaped under the influence and impact of this corpus of racialized, sexualized and ethno-cultural myths. Fire dragon feminism is interested in collecting the women's stories of how they break free of these myths, queer power structures imposed on them and carve out their trailblazing path for collective survival and sustainability. Conducting an autopsy of the archive of myths, fire dragon feminism exposes the various hegemonic systems of patriarchy, sexism, misogyny, coloniality and racial capitalism constricting and restricting life chances of Asian migrant women, shaping their epistemes and ontologies and determining their life-sustaining strategies.

Asian migrant women's implications in global racial capitalist, colonial and neoliberal projects

My late 婆婆 Popo, maternal grandmother (1930–2020) of Indonesian-Peranakan heritage clad in sarong, emigrated to Singapore in 1955 from her hometown, Palembang in South Sumatra province of Indonesia. She was match-made to my late maternal Singaporean ethnic Chinese grandfather in Palembang when the ship that the latter worked on as a seaman docked at Palembang. My grandfather decided to settle down in Palembang with my grandmother and set up a fruit stall to earn a modest living. They had three children in Palembang, and according to my 大姨妈 eldest auntie, 婆婆 Popo was happy living a simple family life in her hometown. But life became hard for her when she had to move to Singapore with her husband and three young children after my grandfather contracted tuberculosis and decided to return to Singapore to seek medical treatment. She went on to give birth to another four children including my mother after immigration (see Figure 2.3). When her two elder children entered the workforce in their teenage years after completing primary school education, she started working

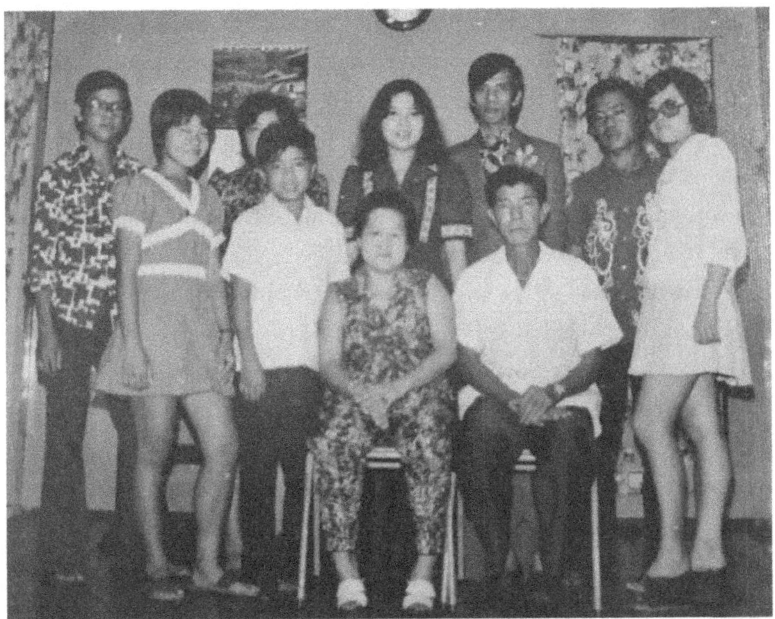

Figure 2.3 My maternal grandmother and family.

as well to supplement household income for a low-income, struggling family of nine. She earned a meagre wage cleaning floors of newly built houses and, later, as a domestic helper working long hours at British, Japanese and Taiwanese expatriate households in late 1950s and 1960s. During one of my trips home, I visited 婆婆 Popo and asked her about her work as a domestic helper. One of the memories that stuck with her was the great difficulty she experienced in her job as a casual ironing lady for a white military household: 'Those military uniforms are very hard to iron … I iron till my hands hurt.' It was during this period that large number of local women were recruited as domestic servants and casual cleaning and laundry ladies at foreign households, particularly British, Australian and New Zealand military households (Twomey 2023). Even though the British colonial period had concluded, the presence of British and its Commonwealth allies remained strong in Malaya and Singapore. The British Commonwealth Far East Strategic Reserve (1955–71) brought thousands of British, Australian and New

Zealander military personnel and their families to work and reside in Malaya and Singapore and employed local women as domestic helpers in their households (Twomey 2023). These white military personnel made no reservation in maintaining the tradition of hiring domestic servants to reinforce white supremacy and class prestige even though the colonial empire had already been dismantled in these parts of the world (Chaudhuri 1994; Sen 2009; Twomey 2023).

In the post-war 1950s and 1960s, local women including my 婆婆 Popo were employed as servants and laundry women. They gradually replaced the China-born *Amahs* and India-born *Ayahs* who were formerly employed in considerable numbers as domestic servants during the nineteenth and twentieth centuries in colonial households in South and Southeast Asia and would follow their employers across Asia, Europe and Australia (Haskins, Banerjee & Lowrie 2021; Twomey 2023). However, households in Singapore returned to the foreign women workforce after the country gained independence in 1965 and ushered local women into her expanding manufacturing and service industries in the late 1960s and 1970s (Huang & Yeoh 2015). My 婆婆 Popo stopped working as a domestic helper when her two older children entered the workforce after completing their primary school education. My oldest Indonesia-born auntie, 大姨妈, another important interlocutor of this research, started working at the age of twelve in 1963, first as a laundry girl washing clothes for several households in the morning and ironing clothes for other households in the afternoon. At the age of fifteen, she worked as a domestic helper, and when she reached the legal age to work in a factory, she too was absorbed into the industrial workforce expanding in late 1960s and 1970s. She subsequently worked in garment, electronics and firearms factories. While local women contribute significantly to the growth of national economy, foreign women are brought in to fill labour gaps in middle-class and upper-class households. Asian migrant women from low-income backgrounds and less wealthy countries in the region, namely the Philippines, Thailand, Sri Lanka, Indonesia, India, Myanmar and Cambodia, are mobilized and employed in large numbers to supply intimate, domestic and care labour to wealthier countries in the region like Singapore (Huang & Yeoh 2015).

The significance of Asian women labour migration in boosting global capitalism and neoliberalism has long been well-documented (for example, Lan 2008; Boris & Parreñas 2010; Parreñas 2014; Radhakrishnan & Solari 2015). I have written in my earlier work (Quah 2020a) as well about the extensive research by transnational feminist scholars on the role feminization of labour plays in the expansion of global neoliberal economy and the extensive mobilization of low-income women from poorer regions in Central and South America, Africa and Asia to meet the demands for intimate, domestic, reproductive and care labour by middle- and upper-class households in wealthier countries (Lan 2008; Boris & Parreñas 2010; Mohanty 2013; Parreñas 2014; Radhakrishnan & Solari 2015). One of the noteworthy contributions made to the scholarly debates on this particular form of extraction of resources in the global racial capitalist and neoliberal economy is by Arlie Hochschild (2003). Hochschild (2003) describes the supply of low-income women for domestic, intimate and care labour as the 'new gold', where wealthier countries around the world are hungry to excavate, extract, expend and dispose. She equates this 'new gold' to the colonial extraction of gold, ivory and rubber from the Third World during the nineteenth century (Hochschild 2003). What is important to note here is that the colonial logic of extraction, dispossession, subjugation and exploitation is hardly something in the past. Former colonial powers made rich by the expansion of their empire go on to dominate global economy with racial capitalist logic and its latest manifestation in the form of neoliberalism and technological dominance. The world continues to turn to the African continent for excavation of raw materials and minerals and Central and South American and Asian countries for labour supply in this US-European dominant economic system. To make sense of how contemporary Asian migrant women's labour and lives have become so critically and intimately implicated in global and transnational neoliberal economies, I turn to scholarly works who have advanced sophisticated debates on racial capitalism and colonialism (e.g., Lowe 2015; Hartman 2019; Gilmore 2020; Robinson 2021).

This book understands race as power relations with its genealogy tracing directly to the expansion of European empire and colonization (Eng & Han 2018). Global histories of race point to the development of categorization and hierarchization of human life into superior, civilized European white race and unruly savages that need to be civilized and educated, which then justify the European colonial empires' dispossession and massacres of Indigenous populations, colonial settlement, transatlantic African slave trade and Asian indentureship. Race and racism are therefore tools used for capital usurpation and amassment. This interwoven relationship between race and capitalism is what Cedric Robinson refers to as racial capitalism (Robinson 2021). Racial capitalism expressed through colonialism and global expansion of colonial empire has subsequently mutated into another perverse form, neoliberalism, while maintaining the same principles of occupation, domination, extraction, dispossession, elimination and subjugation (include reference here on neoliberalism). Race and capitalism reinforce each other and are articulated in various forms, notably through racial nationalism or ethnonationalism (Kazanjian 2006). Ruth Wilson Gilmore (2020) has also reminded us that capitalism requires inequalities and racism enshrines it. What this means is that we cannot silo race without talking about interrelated hegemonies, and we cannot silo class without talking about race. While it appears common sense, an Australian white man class scholar whom I previously worked with was rather insistent on class studies being separate from race analyses as if class and race have nothing to do with each other and they could be treated as individual analytical categories. It is curious how class scholars, in particular dominant class scholars like my former peer, could be resistant in acknowledging the intimate relations between race and class. It is clear that they wilfully ignore the evidence that race has been used by the ruling class and elites to explain their superiority and justify their capital plundering and hoarding historically and in contemporary times. Lisa Lowe (2015) points out that this selective amnesia on colonial violence and collective memory of European liberalism as the key to civilization, freedom and progress have become naturalized in archives of histories. Lowe (2015) writes that the racial capitalist, colonial economy 'civilises and develops freedoms for "man" in modern Europe and North America, while relegating others to geographical and temporal spaces that are constituted as backward, uncivilised and unfree' (2015: 3). Such narratives of cementing European modern liberalism as benchmarks of civility, emancipation and humanity form the foundation of universalized knowledge and education systems. Till today, we continue to put them on the pedestal in different parts of the world, including the formerly colonized worlds. This world order remains unshaken where North America and Western European countries dominate global hierarchies locking the rest of world in political, economic and cultural anxieties over their subordinate positions. Even while Asian and Middle Eastern economies boom, European modern liberal ideals of civility, progress and prosperity stubbornly etch on national and individual psyches in the remaining subordinated, implicated and exploited worlds. Lowe (2015) conceptualizes race as a verb where the ever-shifting process of racialization subjects the world to universalism of European liberal human subject and forgetting of colonial history of empire expansion, Indigenous dispossession, transatlantic slave trade and Asian indentureship.

Agreeing with scholars who have written extensively on the contemporary and interrelated effects of colonialism, racial capitalism, empire and globalization (Robinson 2021; Hartman 2019; Lowe 2015), I posit that we cannot discuss Asian migrant women's implications in contemporary global neoliberal economy without considering the colonial histories that lay the foundation of today's global extraction of resources, hierarchy of nations and uneven distribution of life chances. Colonialism, slavery, empire and indentureship are certainly not something of the past but have continued in different yet similar hierarchal structures of a global neoliberal economy driven by US-European dominance, emerging economies' colonialization of less powerful regions and further extraction and impoverishment of least powerful countries. Continuous and enormous extraction of transnational and intra-national migrant labour plays an indispensable role in the reproduction of the global bourgeois and urban proletariat class and expansion of the global neoliberal economy (Robinson 2021), though individual member of the labour supply is completely dispensable, expendable, disposable and exterminable. Robinson (2021) explains, 'The bourgeois that led the development of capitalism were drawn from particular ethnic and cultural groups [US-European white populations], the European proletariats and the mercenaries of the leading states from others, its peasants from still other cultures, and its slaves from entirely different worlds' (2021: 26). Robinson (2021) adds that this racial capitalism system aims to differentiate, create class hierarchy, assert European supremacy and 'exaggerate regional, subcultural and dialectical differences into "racial ones"' (2021: 26). Accompanying the transatlantic slave trade from the African continent, indentured labour from China and South Asia were imported to buttress the expansion of European colonial empire (Lowe 2015). Racial capitalism forms the framework of colonialism and European imperialism. As part of this deeply entrenched and powerful racial capitalist system, migrant women from less wealthy regions continue to be mobilized in large numbers across the globe form an imperative pool of feminised labour force in providing intimate, domestic and care labour from domestic work, sex work, beauty care, health care, eldercare, hospitality, cleaning to even marriage (Lan 2008; Boris & Parreñas 2010; Mohanty 2013; Parreñas 2014; Radhakrishnan & Solari 2015; Quah 2020a).

To explain my and other women's troubles as a racialized and sexualized Asian migrant woman employee at the epicentre of white supremacy training, it is pertinent to explain the broader and interrelated contexts of racialization of Asian migrant women in the past and present. Following the scholarly directions of Lisa Lowe (2015), who show the intimate connections and interdependencies between the colonial expansion of the empire, settler-colonialism, transatlantic slave trade and Chinese and South Asian indentureship, this book seeks to account for the interconnected contexts of racialization of Asian migrant women during the colonial period, the colonial legacy of racialization and sexualization contemporary Asian migrant women have come to inherit and the continuous racialization and sexualization they are subjected to in present neoliberal projects. While it is important to give weight to the discrimination and victimization Asian migrant women encounter and explain the various contexts their encounters occur, it is also really urgent to acknowledge their implications, participation and complicity in the expansion of global neoliberal economy. Asian migrant women are implicated in expanding ambitious neoliberal projects and therefore not spared from being complicit in dispossessing Indigenous peoples and local communities, strengthening racial capitalist, colonial and neoliberal logics of resource theft, appropriation, extraction and hoarding, fuelling global inequalities and contributing directly to racialization of less powerful peoples and even self-racialization.

For example, we cannot ignore the elephant in the room – the rising dominance of China. The discussion needs to include the contradictions of benefitting from unearned racial capital and, at the same time, being culpable in the racialization and oppression of less powerful Indigenous peoples. Scholars have delved into China's economic expansion in Africa, Pacific Islands and Southeast Asia raising questions about China's colonialization of these regions and the less desirable effects of Chinese neoliberal projects on local populations (Antwi-Boateng 2017; Bodomo 2018; Kleven 2019; Calabrese & Wang 2023). China's ambitious Belt and Road Initiative has seen to the ravaging excavation of raw materials including minerals, fossil fuels and agricultural produces for their manufacturing industries, which in turn operate in full gear to feed the insatiable demands of the rest of the world all hankering after 'Made in China' products (Kleven 2019). Especially in the continent of Africa, China's sprawling Belt and Road projects mark their dominance in thirty-nine countries, not just in the economic sphere but their strong influence includes military expansion with the setting of military bases and political interference in national governance (Risberg 2019).

China's colonization projects also sprawl across the Pacific Islands including Vanuatu, Papua New Guinea, Solomon Islands, Fiji, Tonga and Nauru (Smith & Wesley-Smith 2021), as well as Southeast Asian countries. For example, in Cambodia, Sihanoukville is notorious for being a wonderland for Chinese investors, particularly gambling and property industries. The ban of casino gambling in China brings Chinese investors to set up casinos in Southeast Asia and Chinese gamblers to these places. In Sihanoukville, a 'Chinese silo' has been created where Chinese investors seem to get a free rein in property development and tourism and gambling industry with limited regulatory oversight by the Cambodian government (Calabrese & Wang 2023). The lack of regulations has led to mushrooming of disasters such as building collapses leading to deaths and criminality including murder, money laundering, kidnapping and violent gun attacks (Calabrese & Wang 2023; Tappe & Rowedder 2023). In a documentary by Al Jazeera's 101 East(2019), a particular scene where an organized group of Chinese business tourists flashing their banner, 'High level business visit: digging for gold in Cambodia', set out to find investment opportunities is especially telling of their excavation and extraction pursuits. One of them commented that Cambodia reminded him of China ten years ago, and 'China is helping Cambodia in so many ways, in infrastructure, construction and so many ways … I think Cambodia depends on China a lot … we don't see this as a problem, we see this as an opportunity.' Another Chinese entrepreneur featured in the documentary indicated that China's Belt and Road Initiative was a good way for China to deliver and share their good technology and cultures to different countries, and when the project was done, we would see a beautiful city at Sihanoukville.

Since its inception, China's Belt and Road Initiative has been aggressively pursuing its global capitalist and neoliberal projects at the expense of less powerful but resource-rich countries. While the United States and its allies including the UK and Australia are quick to criticize and raise concerns over China's colonialism projects in Africa and the Pacific Islands, it is not hard to see the hypocrisy especially when what China is doing now is emulating the neoliberal model that the United States and UK came up with in the 1970s. One cannot help but notice the eerie yet unsurprising similarity between Euro-American and Chinese colonialisms. Creating a racial hierarchy of humanity to assert racial superiority and justify extraction, disguising pillaging with saviourhood and leaving a trail of devastation appears to be the blueprint of China's colonialization as we witness. That is exactly the blueprint of racial capitalism and imperialism European colonizers used in the nineteenth and twentieth centuries. It is also the blueprint of Americanization the United States employed since the Cold War. To be fair, this racial capitalist blueprint is not only adopted by China but also by other powerful players including former colonial powers in the global neoliberal economy. Scholars have pointed out that dominance by power players including the United States, UK and China could be better explained as neocolonialism where the state concerned, in theory, is an independent sovereignty but its political governance and economic policy are controlled by more powerful countries (Kwame 1965). China may have differed in their neocolonial tactics, for example, void of territorial control and settler-colonial, and use of soft power instead of direct interference, as compared to their European colonial predecessors (Antwi-Boateng 2017). However, the colonial logic of extraction, dispossession and exploitation, motivation and agenda of resource amassment and wealth gain through taking from local communities and employment of altruism narrative to justify assertion of power remain intact in the colonial or neocolonial blueprint.

Even when China sees the United States as its ultimate nemesis and embarks on such a large-scale Chinese ethno-nationalistic endeavour, the Belt and Road Initiative, to be a stronger economic player than the United States, they ironically and sadly mimic the American model to a tee. At the same time as China zealously shouts Chinese pride and urges their Chinese peoples to follow the China Dream – to be wealthy, to be powerful and to be respected (Wang 2014) – it is unfortunate that the United States is still used as the point of reference in every fibre of the Chinese national and sociocultural psyche therefore reinforcing American imperialism and paying their American opponent the greatest compliment. Audre Lorde's words came to mind: 'American standards are sort of an unspoken norm, and that whether one resists them, or whether one adopts them, they are there to be reckoned with. This is rather disappointing' (Lorde 2019: 8). Lorde's observation about omnipresent Americanism during her visit to Moscow, Russia, in 1976 appears to still ring true, more notably observed in today's rising China.

What all these means is that being entangled in a web of myths and realities in intimately interconnected worlds, Asian migrant women reap racial and economic privileges and are typecast as the rich Asian or Chinese or Indian with the emergence of rising Asian economies, particularly China's Belt and Road Initiative. At the same time, Asian migrant women undoubtedly suffer collateral damage with heightened Sinophobia due to China's increasing dominance, anti-Asian hate due to recent Covid-19 pandemic fuelled racism wave, Islamophobia due to residual effects of 9/11 attacks in the United States and Israel's colonization of Palestine abetted by the United States and their allies including Australia. However, they cannot be absolved of culpability in contributing to racial capitalist, neoliberal and colonial projects that dispossess, disenfranchise and debilitate less powerful peoples. We are extracted and expended, but we extract and expend too. We cannot simply lean towards the victimization narrative where Asian migrant women are subjected to racism or the agency advocacy propping Asian migrant women up as autonomous, brave and strong subjects capable of overcoming challenges and emerging as well-adjusted migrants, successful entrepreneurs and productive citizens. Neither can we rely on the Dragon Lady portrayal demonizing the women as greedy family wreckers and scheming mail-order brides. Instead of further entrapping the women in these singular, racializing frames, how can we more comprehensively understand the interconnected structures that shape their involvements, encounters, challenges and responsibilities? What does it mean to be racialized, extracted and ornamentalized while racializing, appropriating and exploiting others for capital gain? What does it mean to be advantaged and injured at the same time by racializing myths of prosperity and debauchery the women have come to be associated with? More importantly, what kind of feminist politics and strategies can we employ to break free of such seemingly inescapable cages so that we may all survive and thrive?

Asian migrant women's implications in white settler-colonial Australian society

This book considers the white settler-colonial Australian society as its field site of study. The project is interested to turn to Asian migrant women's entanglements with myths and realities in white Australian settler-colonial society and explore how their stories help us think more broadly about shifting migrant positionality, trajectory and strategy and develop migrant feminist ethics to address their privileges, complicity and responsibilities in global colonial, racial capitalist and neoliberal projects. To provide the context, there were over 7.6 million migrants living in Australia and about 30 per cent of Australia's population were born overseas according to official statistics collected during 2019–20 (ABS 2021). Other than those born in England being the largest group of overseas-born migrant residents living in Australia, India-born and China-born migrant residents take the second and third place (ABS 2021). Asian countries including The Philippines, Vietnam, Malaysia and Sri Lanka are also on the list of top ten migrant source countries (ABS 2021). In 2019–20, overseas migrant arrivals from Asian region including Southeast, Northeast, South and Central Asia occupy 54 per cent of the total number of overseas migrant arrivals in Australia (ABS 2021). Before 1981, the ten largest overseas-born migrant groups in Sydney did not include a single Asian country source (Hugo & Harris 2011). However, by 2006, Sydney's top ten largest overseas-born migrant groups include China-born, India-born, Vietnam-born, The

Philippines-born, Hong Kong-born and South Korea-born migrant residents (Hugo & Harris 2011).

Australian immigration policy has not always been this hospitable to immigrants from Asian region. The racially biased White Australia Policy with its Immigration Restriction Act (1901–58) saw the exclusion of non-European immigrants and inclusion of European immigrants from Eastern and Central Europe and the Baltic region previously seen as 'not white enough'. The post-war 1940s and 1950s immigration policy emphasized assimilation where immigrants were expected to be Australian through speaking English and living by Australian values. In the 1960s and 1970s, the Australian government policy gradually moved from assimilation to integration to multiculturalism 'in recognition of the challenges facing migrants in settling into Australian society and acceptance that new arrivals may not want to lose their cultural identity' (Koleth 2010: 4). On the surface, it appeared that the nation state's border control policy has moved towards a more humanitarian and hospitable approach in handling immigrants. But the longevity and resilience of colonial division of humanity could still be observed in our contemporary neoliberal worlds operating on an exclusion/inclusion principle with the majority hoarding capital, deciding who gets access and how much access they could have, excluding those who are deemed unqualified and undeserving of their benevolence and including those who have been evaluated to possess productive value and potential and express zealousness in assimilating and be more like them (Lowe 2015). The Whitlam government finally put the racist White Australia Policy to an end in 1972 and brought about the official inception of multiculturalism policy in 1973 paying more attention to the settlement and welfare issues of immigrants (Koleth 2010). Australian immigration policy turned more welcoming to non-European immigrants. In 1975, the Australian government introduced the Racial Discrimination Act to fulfil its obligations to the International Convention of the Elimination of All Forms of Racial Discrimination (1969), hence making all forms of racial discrimination including race-based immigration policy illegal (Koleth 2010). While racial discrimination is prohibited by law, racism and xenophobia arguably prevail in the everyday life and psyches of Australian society. One could observe their manifestations in colour-blind disguise where the nation state implemented official celebration of its self-congratulatory, successful integration of migrants on Multicultural Day and later Harmony Day since 1999 or in the ghost of colonialism where Aboriginal and Torres Strait Islanders were only granted citizenship on their own lands in 1967 and the life outcomes gap between Indigenous and non-Indigenous populations remains stark (Blackwell 2024), or out in plain view with blatant fearmongering, scapegoating and prejudice-inciting public and political discourses on perceived threats of 'Asianization' (Jayasuriya & Kee 2013), 'Islamic radicalization' (Askarzai 2022), 'African gangs' (Moran 2022), just to name a few examples. Archer et al. (2022) also argue that despite Australian state's multiculturalism policy and rhetoric, 'the "bodies", both physical and social, of Women of Colour continue to be "othered" through sexual objectification, xenophobia, and racism, with the recent and historic colonial past of Australia setting up Women of Colour as the other – to cis-gendered men, as well as to heteronormative, white women' (2022: 826).

While there have been considerable scholarly works on Asian American women, less research has been done on Asian migrant women in the other end of the world, Australia. For example, Australian historians have conceded the difficulty in obtaining records of early Chinese migrant women in Australia as 'Chinese Australian history is primarily told as a history of men' (Bagnall & Martinez 2021). The lack of records in the archive is first and foremost a result of low numbers of Chinese migrant women then where 'in 1901, there were almost 30,000 Chinese men in Australia, yet fewer than 500 women' (Bagnall & Martinez 2021). Most of the Chinese migrant women in Australia during the nineteenth and early twentieth centuries were mainly wives who moved from the rural Pearl River Delta region in the Guangdong province to join their Chinese labourer husbands who have migrated earlier, or daughters, or accompanying servants (Bagnall & Martinez 2021; Lowrie 2021). The Chinese domestic servants clad in black pants and white blouse are known as the black and white *Amahs* or 妈姐 *Majie* from organized spinster sisterhood groups originated in China (Lowrie 2021). The reasons for the low numbers of Chinese migrant women in Australia during that British colonial period were two-pronged: the Chinese government wanted the women to stay behind to look after the households while the men emigrated for economic opportunities and the White Australia Policy's anti-Asian immigration laws were determined to keep Chinese women out (Bagnall & Martinez 2021). According to historical records, more Chinese *Amahs* arrived in Australia just before the Second World War when they moved with their evacuated British employers from Hong Kong, Singapore and Malaya (Lowrie 2021). However, they were not allowed to stay on after the war ended and were forced out under the White Australia Policy's Immigration Restriction Act (1901–58) (Lowrie 2021). Similarly, there was also a low number of Indian immigrant women during the colonial period. Most of them travelled with their British employers as domestic servants known as *Ayahs*. The earliest historical records of *Ayahs* in Australia show that the first three *Ayahs* arrived in Sydney, New South Wales, in 1818 with the Browne household from Kolkata (Haskins 2021). When William Browne with half British and half Indian heritage was welcomed and offered land by the then governor, Lachlan Macquarie, he brought with him his wife and several Indian man and woman servants (Haskins 2021). What the archives present is that the Chinese and Indian migrant women were never quite settled and rooted in one particular place but rather transient as they travelled with their colonial British employers between Britain, India, China, Hong Kong, Singapore, Malaya and Australia. Occupying a lower socio-economic background during the colonial period as a domestic servant or accompanying wife of indentured labourers or independent labourers, Asian migrant women have been subjected to racialization, sexualization and othering since then and continue to inherit such colonial legacy.

However, it is also important to note that the Chinese *Amahs* and Indian *Ayahs* were directly implicated in the reproduction of colonial households through the supply of their domestic and intimate labour as servants hired by British colonialists and their Commonwealth allies. Early Asian women migrant-settlers who moved to Australia as accompanying wives instead of servants were also directly involved in settler-colonialism projects dispossessing Indigenous peoples, grabbing lands and plundering resources when they supported their migrant businessmen or labourer husbands in the reproduction of their settler households. The subsequent waves of immigration that brought Asian immigrant women to Australia continually played a vital role in Australian settler-colonialism and dispossession of Aboriginal and Torres Strait Islander peoples. The introduction of points-based immigration system in the 1970s coinciding with the Whitlam government's multiculturalism policy brought in skilled migrants with qualifications that meet labour needs of Australian economy (Jupp 2007; Koleth 2015). The points-based migrant selection system creates a quantifiable human value evaluation formula to determine the productive capital and potential an immigration applicant has and ensures that the migrant candidates selected and approved to enter are less likely to be on the dough and be a welfare burden to the Australian economy (Jupp 2007; Koleth 2015). In line with the colonial legacy of divisions of humanity and the rest of the world's racial capitalist economies, Australian immigration policy has since been operating based on neoliberal logics to rank and value humanity according to productive capital, reproductive potential, as well as financial independence with minimal reliability. Australian multiculturalism policy more importantly supports the diversity of workforce skills and businesses needed in growing Australian economic developments in the global market (Murphy et al. 2003; Koleth 2015). With this points-based immigration application system, Asian immigrant women like the rest of the Australian immigrant pool are evaluated according to their productive and reproductive value and potential. In the 1970s and 1980s, Asian immigrant women were mainly family stream migrants where they were the secondary applicants or dependent applicants accompanying their husbands who were the primary skilled migrant applicants. However, from the 1990s, this appeared to have changed. A research study conducted in late 1990s shows that Asian immigrant women in Australia were not just passive, accompanying wives but some of whom were entrepreneurs who either started their own business in Australia or entered a partnership as an equal partner (Ip & Lever-Tracy 1999). The project's findings point to their trailblazing and gung ho entrepreneurship where they started new businesses and had their husbands quit their jobs to join them in their enterprises (Ip & Lever-Tracy 1999). According to the 2001 Population and Housing Census of Australia, one-third migrant women aged between fifteen and fifty-four in Australia were from Asian region (Foroutan & Mcdonald 2008). More than half of the cohort emigrated from Southeast Asian countries; most of the Southeast Asian immigrant women were Vietnamese and Filipino with the rest from Malaysia, Indonesia, Singapore, Thailand and Cambodia (Foroutan & Mcdonald 2008). About one-third of the Asian immigrant women emigrated from Central and North East Asia; the majority of this group moved from China and Mongolia and the rest were from Iraq, Iran and Afghanistan (Foroutan & Mcdonald 2008). About 15 per cent of the Asian immigrant women recorded in the 2001 population census were South Asian women mainly from India and Sri Lanka with the rest from Pakistan and Bangladesh (Foroutan & Mcdonald 2008). The study notes that more than half of the whole cohort of Asian immigrant women were employed and a third of them were in professional and managerial positions (Foroutan & Mcdonald 2008). The immigration trends changed subsequently with immigrants from India and China surpassing other Asian countries, and in fact, India-born and China-born immigrants take the second and third places of the total overseas-born populations in Australia according to official statistics collected in 2019–20 (ABS 2021). What is important to note is that between 2009 and 2015, the majority of immigrant women among the first four source countries, India, China, the UK and the Philippines, were primary applicant-independent skilled immigrants rather than secondary applicant-family stream immigrants (Carangio et al. 2021). Among the Asian skilled immigrant women,

Indian migrant women formed the largest group, followed by Chinese and the Filipino (Carangio et al. 2021) women. The number of skilled immigrant women also exceeded family immigrant women during the reference period of 2009–2015 (Carangio et al. 2021). It is clear that Asian women skilled immigrants and entrepreneurs play a significant contributory role in the growth of Australian settler-colonial workforce and economy.

The productive value and potential attached to Asian immigrant women, while elevating their socio-economic positions in Australian society, also reinforces their racialization as model minority and desirable citizens. Ien Ang (1996) in her article 'The Curse of the Smile' writes how Asian women were portrayed as desirable candidates for Australian government's immigration and citizenship campaign in the 1990s. She describes a government poster featuring an Asian-presenting woman with the caption, 'Come and join our family' that aimed to encourage migrant residents to take up Australian citizenship. She interestingly points out that what the government poster was conveying strongly was that the Asian migrant woman was presented and promoted as the ideal migrant resident candidate that the Australian state would like to recruit into their Australian family. This reinforces Anne Anlin Cheng's (2019) provocation on how Asiatic femininity is appropriated for the making of white personhood and strengthening white dominance. The Asian woman's ornamental Asiatic feminine value is key here in the making of white superior race whereby her aestheticization and ornamentalization make her palatable, non-threatening, accommodating and gentle in the white Australian nationhood project. The Asian migrant woman is the light version of multiculturalism that the white Australian state and people could stomach. Ang (1996) argues the Australian multiculturalism project has relegated the Asian migrant woman to a grey, ambivalent space of almost being included but not quite. The Asian migrant woman is included by the white dominator because of her consigned exotic, aesthetic and ornamental Asiatic feminine value, and it is precisely this portrayal that makes her a desirable, acceptable and 'not scary' family member that the expanding white Australian family is willing to adopt (Ang 1996). The Asian woman is desirable because she is visibly and culturally different from the white dominator, and it is exactly this difference that renders her significant value in the Australian state's multiculturalism project and corporations' cultural diversity efforts. She is supposed to be different so that her permitted inclusion signals Australian multiculturalism. But her desirability also hinges upon her perceived non-threatening, palatable and intelligible difference where the white dominator could tolerate and accept. Ang (1996) points out that however heterogeneous Asian migrant women are, we all share 'the curse of the smile' (1996: 48), where we have all been imposed with the expectation of keeping our smile on, playing up our ornamental role in profiling cultural exoticism, ignoring racialization process, learning to assimilate and blend in with the whiteness, displaying gratitude for being let in by the white majority and celebrating Australian multiculturalism with our culturally exotic food and aesthetic cultural clothes.

Ang (1996) laments over her realization that she is the 'desired other', and her 'femininity actually enhances that desirability' in Australian multiculturalism landscape (1996: 46). She especially notes that her other attributes like speaking English fluently and being a highly educated academic make her 'Western' enough and therefore a model citizen with not just cultural but also economic value in the Australian society (Ang 1996). This appears to be an advantageous combination for Asian migrant women. Like Ien Ang, I tick these boxes of desirability and even tick an additional box of LGBTIQA+ diversity to signal Western modernity and add more points to white palatability. A queer Singapore national, ethnic Chinese migrant queer woman academic like me was especially sought after by the 2023 Sydney World Pride events to showcase cultural representation and so-called intersectional diversity in an otherwise vanilla-white Australian queer landscape. Importantly, what cannot be omitted in this discussion is the racial hierarchy in the region. Clearly, not all Asian immigrants are deemed as desirable symbols of Australian multiculturalism. Certain Asian nationalities and cultures are prized more than others. For example, it is hard to ignore how the Lunar New Year and the 2024 Year of Dragon are more widely celebrated at Australian retail outlets, art centres, public libraries and schools compared to other cultural festivals such as Diwali (Hindu's Festival of Light) and Nowruz (Persian New Year) celebrated by their large, diverse Asian immigrant populations. The Australian's New South Wales Government even provides Lunar New Year commemorative birth certificates and on its website, a promotional description for Year of Dragon reads, 'The Dragon is one of the most sought-after Chinese zodiac signs, representing luck, strength, and wealth and is a fitting honour for anyone lucky enough to be born or adopted during this powerful Lunar Year' (NSW 2024). Ultimately, this is the problem with 'inclusion/exclusion' and identity representation politics, where the master decides who gets included and who remains at the fringe, and the master remains in charge and powerful. Such politics result in less powerful peoples existing according to the master's logic and unequal power dynamics remaining undisrupted (Quah 2023). Based on the white dominator's terms of inclusion, the Asian migrant woman must remain aesthetic and ornamental as the pretty and smiling poster child for Australian multiculturalism and cultural diversity promotion campaigns. White people are happy with Asian immigrant women like me as long as we know our place and learn to be white, *but not too white* till we let it get into our pretty heads that we are equal to them and start picking up their white habits of freedom of speech, feminism and social justice activism. This is when I got into troubles – big troubles. I crossed the line white people had drawn for me and was punished severely for daring to transgress. In this study, I found other Asian migrant women who ran into similar troubles like me.

Why another strand of feminism?

The historical records attest that even during the British colonial period, the Chinese *Amahs* and Indian *Ayahs* did not meekly take in the beatings, ill-treatments and exploitative work conditions. On the contrary, while being rendered powerless in a colonial system of domestic servanthood and racial hierarchy of white superiority, they did not go down quietly without a fight. We got a glimpse of their feminist activisms when they resisted against their colonial masters and organized themselves through unions to fight for better work conditions. One of the first *Ayahs* to arrive in Australia in 1818 with the Browne ship from India, Thomassee, having faced beatings and serious abuse working with the Browne household, conspired with her two fellow ayah co-workers and sent the then local governor a joint memorial of complaint (Haskins 2021). They requested to be released from the bondage of slavery and sent back to India (Haskins 2021). The Browne couple was also found ill-treating their other Indian servants and the case including the *Ayahs'* petition was brought before the magistrates in 1819 (Merani & Gonsalves 2019; Haskins 2021). The magistrates ruled in favour of the Indian servants and ordered William Browne to release all his forty Indian servants of their bondage (Haskins 2021). The *Ayahs'* joint memorial was subsequently included in the report on slavery in East India presented to the British House of Commons in 1827 (Haskins 2021). Besides the Indian *Ayahs*, the Chinese *Amahs* also organized themselves to fight for better work rights and conditions (Lowrie 2021; Twomey 2023). The Chinese *Amahs* were known for their independence and strong sisterhood networks formed through lodging houses (Twomey 2023). When the Chinese *Amahs* moved from Hong Kong to Australia with their evacuated British colonizer households between 1940 and 1942, they negotiated their employment and relocation based on their own terms through *Amahs'* union (Lowrie 2021). In subsequent decades, their organization through *Amahs'* unions remained robust in former colonies. For example, in 1963, three thousand *Amahs* in Malaya voted through their union to go on strike in protest of the plan to transfer them from public employment under government contracts to private employment with individual British Commonwealth servicemen (Twomey 2023).

These early migrant women arguably defy the myths of obedient, meek and powerless Asian women servants, and while being hardworking heavyweights in colonial and subsequent nationalist projects, their accounts have proven that they are feminist activists in their own ways to fight for survival and fairer work conditions against colonialism and capitalist exploitation. I think of my 婆婆 Popo, my maternal grandmother who had in her life inconsistently displayed obstinate, fiery matriarchy against patriarchy and toxic masculinity pronounced in the familial space. Her feminist stance was, in my opinion, beautifully and powerfully inarticulate and incoherent. She moved across Malacca Strait from Palembang to Chinese-dominant Singapore in her Peranakan sarong and faced discrimination for not being Chinese enough because of her Peranakan cladding. She worked as a domestic servant at colonial and expatriate households to supplement family income, reared her seven children almost singlehandedly, stayed legally married but 'lived together apart' from estranged husband. Through it all, she held onto her matriarchal position earning deep respect and fond affection from her offsprings and theirs. Her story is not exceptional though. It is important to note that recognizing the women's including my 婆婆 Popo's feminist activism is not to idealize or immortalize them and absolve their responsibilities in the growth of colonialism and racial capitalism. However, what is noteworthy is that these Asian migrant women, in their own courageous, clever and, at the same time, contradictory and complicit ways, wiggle to break free of imposing myths and strive for more sustainable realities and futures for themselves and others, hence allowing other women to stand on their shoulders and keep carrying on with the feminist ploughing.

In the context of North American society, Anne Anlin Cheng (2019) posits that the yellow woman, Asian American women and Asian feminism have not been given sufficient scholarly attention as compared to white feminism, liberal feminism and Black feminism. She argues the yellow woman is often the 'ghost in the machine' left untheorized and neglected in the discussion and critique of Western, white, masculine, agentic, individualistic and modern personhood. Mythologized as well-adjusted, compliant, diligent, cooperative, successful and privileged model minority and good citizens, Asian American women neither warrant sufficient sympathy vote to activate white saviourhood and benevolence nor summon adequate whiteness to access platforms and garner attention like their white peers. Cheng (2019) asks an important question here: 'What does it mean to survive as someone too aestheticized to suffer injury but so aestheticized that she invites injury?' (2019: xi). Her conceptualization of ornamentalism is helpful to explain the yellow woman's ornamental Asiatic femininity and her equally important role as the black enslaved body in constructing and sustaining white male personhood. Cheng (2019) brings to our attention 'a different kind of flesh in the history of race making' (2019: 3) and uses ornamental personhood to explain the role the yellow woman plays in the making of modern white man personhood. The ornamentalization of the yellow woman and invisibilization of such ornamentalization is the problem worth attending to. This 'not quite visible and acknowledged' yet occupying a pertinent and productive position in Western personhood is what fire dragon feminism is interested to use as a point of departure and unpack the racialization of Asian migrant women in other parts of the world. Specifically, Cheng's (2019) framework of ornamental personhood of Asiatic femininity is of great value in understanding the yellow woman's race relations with racialized white and Black people and their active involvement and complicity in self-racialization and gatekeeping of whiteness.

There has been a rich body of scholarly works developed on various forms of Asian feminism based on different historical, political, socio-economic and activism contexts. A corpus of important discussions on Asian American women's concerns and activisms has been widely circulated. This is not surprising since global knowledge production and dominance have largely been US-Eurocentric. Nevertheless, significant theorizations on Asian American women and feminism emerged decades ago, for example, Sonia Shah's (1997) *Dragon ladies: Asian American feminists breathe fire* edited collection of sixteen essays featuring everyday racism and sexism, grassroots activism and critiques of white feminism to later works such as *Asian American feminisms and women of color politics* edited by Lynn Fujiwara and Shireen

Roshanravan (2018) and Anne Anlin Cheng's (2019) *Ornamentalism* to the most recent works in relation to pandemic-related anti-Asian racism, for example, Bao Lo's (2023) *Anti-Asian violence and abolition feminism as Asian American feminist praxis.* This body of works is instrumental in attending to the often overlooked and uniquely positioned constituent – the yellow woman in white settler-colonial North American society. Asian American feminisms are useful in many ways in explaining the various historical, political and economic contexts behind racialization myths associated with Asian American women including derogatory sexualized characterizations and model minority stereotypes popularized by US media and Hollywood. It is, however, necessary to differentiate this corpus from another vibrant body of literature that focuses on feminisms in Asian region itself and develops theories about Asian feminisms from Asia. Some of the highly exciting and valuable accounts on grassroots, anti-colonial, Indigenous and transnational feminisms in Asian region include, emphatically not limited to, women's movements across a sample of Asian countries (Roces & Edwards 2010); South Asian feminisms (Loomba & Lukose 2012; Roy 2012); Chinese feminisms in People's Republic of China, Hong Kong and Taiwan (Chang 2009; Chen 2011; Hong Fincher 2018); Islamic feminisms (Ahmed-Ghosh 2015); Southeast Asian feminisms (Katjasungkana & Wieringa 2012; Bong 2016); feminism in Malaysia (Ng, Mohammad & Tan 2006); feminism in Singapore (Lyons 2004). Feminisms from the Asian region are equally key in showcasing place-based, grassroots resistance efforts in specific contexts of colonial histories, geopolitics, national agendas and local sociocultural environments.

I launched my own strand of feminism in the epilogue of my second book, *Transnational divorce: Understanding inequalities and intimacies from Singapore* (Quah 2020a). I have since developed fire dragon feminism in relation to racism, anti-racism and emotional strategies in another piece of writing, *Navigating emotions at the site of racism: feminist rage, queer pessimism and fire dragon feminism* (Quah 2020b). After uncovering many life stories on destructive effects of racial capitalism, global neoliberalism, heteronormativity, patriarchy, sexism, queerphobia and other structural inequalities for more than a decade, I came to a pause in 2020. Inflicted with post-traumatic stress disorder and burnt out, I needed to re-orientate and reconsider my strategies in this feminist resistance work. I needed a clearly defined feminist methodology to give me a firmer grounding amid heightening chaos, instability and violence. I needed a sturdy life buoy to keep me from sinking and being engulfed by tidal waves of heartaches whenever I listened to difficult stories and observed debilitations. I needed a confusion-proof compass to help me orientate and move in affirmative and restorative directions whenever I was torn between persevering with the cause and chasing profitable markers of capitalism-defined success. I needed a durable armour to shield me from life-choking forces set out to cause injury and silence dissent. Up to that point, I have been borrowing tools, strategies and philosophies from anticolonial, transnational, intersectional and queer feminist philosophies and theories including but not limited to the works of Audre Lorde, bell hooks, Toni Morrison, Angela Davis, Gloria Anzaldúa, Maxine Hong Kingston, Ruth Wilson Gilmore, Chandra Talpade Mohanty, Saidiya Hartman, Jasbir Puar, Aileen Robinson-Moreton, Sara Ahmed and others who have profoundly influenced my own feminist positions and methodologies. These powerful and influential feminist writer-teacher-activist women of colour have taught, influenced and inspired me significantly and oftentimes made me feel less alone in the fight. However, I am at the same time oddly alienated by and uneasy with the contextual specificities that set me apart from these feminist scholars I so admire. The historical, political and cultural specificities each feminist writer is located in gave birth to the particular feminist philosophies they uphold, causes they advocate and resistance strategies they employ. My epistemological and ontological positions as a descendant of migrant families and as a migrant myself in my adult life call for a particular strand of feminism that I could relate to, draw strength from and anchor myself in. The epilogue of my second book marks the beginning of my lifelong fire dragon feminist journey.

Fire dragon feminism as lifelong, in-progress, everyday revolutionary project

Fire dragon feminism contributes to these two broad categories of Asian feminisms – Asian American feminism and Asian feminisms from Asia. Fire dragon feminism draws knowledges from Asian American feminisms and feminisms emerging from Asian region to further conceptualize migrant feminism that is not necessarily rooted in any particular place but yet influenced by a myriad of settler-colonial, global racial capitalist and neoliberal, transnational geopolitical, and local historical, political, economic and sociocultural contexts. Fire dragon feminism is concerned with a positionality, ontology, epistemology and ethics that are not rooted in any particular place but are migratory, transnational, interrelated and relational. In particular, it is interested in diasporic Asian women's dynamic migrant histories, positions, epistemes and ontologies in their receiving white, settler-colonial society, as well as their transnational ties, resources, remittances and activisms for survival and collective solidarity. The racialization, sexualization, minoritization, objectification and ornamentalization of Asian migrant women in white Australian settler-colonial society are arguably comparable to the experiences of Asian migrant women in white North American settler-colonial society. At the same time, there is more to the story. Fire dragon feminism is therefore keen in finding out the ways in which Asian migrant women who are not rooted in any centre, not even Australian society, are dispersed, migratory, transnational and international. What kind of feminisms do these Asian migrant women develop and use from nowhere and everywhere?

The significance of fire dragon feminism is not just about offering a case study based on stories of Asian migrant women living and working in white settler-colonial Australian society to the rich global archives of migrant women's stories but also doing a race relations autopsy of structural conditions migrant women with no specific rootedness in any centre live under. To clarify, there is certainly great value in documenting oral accounts of women who have encountered racialization and violence as a political tool to counter wilful institutional amnesia and censorship. Fire dragon feminism is invested in this work of documenting for indictment and correction.

Beyond that, fire dragon feminism's mission is to develop more concrete theorizations on migrant feminism, a distinct form of feminism that speaks to the shifting and intertwined positions of privilege, power, capital, life chances, complicity and responsibilities migrant women hold. Fire dragon feminism is interested in these two propositions: How do we make sense of Asian migrant women's epistemological and ontological positions with their inheritance of racial and colonial legacies, transnational relations and collectives and local implications in white settler-colonial host society? How may we build collective solidarities in the midst of place-based specificities and differences where we are simultaneously racialised by and benefiting from global colonial racial capitalist and neoliberal projects? Fire dragon feminism continually draws theories from migrant women's transnational encounters with coloniality, racial capitalism and neoliberalism. It examines migrant women's implications, privileges and complicity in global colonial and neoliberal projects, as well as their responsibilities, strategies and ethics in denouncing extractive and exploitative forces, changing rules and building solidarity for more sustainable and just futures.

I have written in my earlier works (2020a, 2020b & 2021) that fire dragon feminism is a lifelong, work-in-progress, never finished feminist project that has already been set in motion as I stumble, grow, err and learn till I die. This book is yet another continuation of ongoing excavation, discovery, mapping, shaping and articulation of the philosophies and methodologies I employ to navigate life, relate to others and the environments and carry out different forms of community engagement work. For this particular fire dragon feminist project, I am interested to discuss the myths imposed on Asian migrant women, the implications of such myths in their migrant lives, the differences between the myths and their realities and their revolutionary efforts in breaking free of the myths. As I have explained in the earlier section, the use of the mythical creature, fire dragon is to draw attention to the symbolic and man-made (literally, patriarchal, not just artificial) meanings attached to Asian migrant women. Whether it is Fire Dragon, Dragon Lady or Little Dragon Maiden, Asian women have been associated with a range of socially constructed portrayals and expectations, both uplifting and derogatory. Their stories in the next two chapters will reveal how they at times accept and reinforce these myths, at times collaborate to impose the myths on themselves and others, and at times defy the myths. What fire dragon feminist ethics call for is for Asian migrant women to be introspective and reflective of the colonial legacy and accompanying power, capital and privileges we have come to inherit that advantage and enrich us; our continuing participation and contribution to the growth of racial capitalism and neoliberalism that persist in dispossessing Indigenous peoples, disenfranchising exploited populations and entrapping us in the racialization process; our responsibilities in denouncing, disinvesting, abolishing and revolutionizing for more liveable and sustainable futures where we all, not some, may survive and thrive. The seemingly meek, gentle and compliant Asian migrant women are oftentimes not expected to bite back, revolt and disobey. Some of the women's stories I have the privilege to listen to and collect show that they are unlikely, gutsy revolutionaries in dominant white spaces. Fire dragon feminism is an open provocation to fellow feminists, thinkers, teachers, activists and readers to confront head-on the ornamentalization, exoticization, extraction, commodification, co-optation and invisibilization of Asian migrant women, as well as the latter's quiet compliance and complicit accumulation of capital. It is a lifelong invitation to think and strategize alongside to change the rules for a more liveable existence.

3

Racialized myths and realities of Asian migrant women in the Australian academy

I attempted suicide because I came to an ultimate point of despair and hopelessness. If I cannot fight against the system and am so crushed, debilitated and destroyed by the white oppressive machinery … and there is nothing I could do anymore to seek redress … and I am being so heavily punished by every possible mechanism of the racist machinery without any chance of defence and escape … and without an ounce of hope for redress and justice, how do I carry on doing this work? How can I teach what I teach in class and tell my students that we can make this world a better place? How can I tell them there is hope for this world to have justice and equality when I no longer see hope? I reached a point of total despondence and did not see how I could carry on in spite of what everyone was telling me.

This short excerpt is taken from the notes I wrote earlier on my deep sadness and trauma stemmed from the assault of racism and whiteness I had encountered in the Australian academy. Official messages promoting the myth of meritocracy and equality constantly flood our sensibilities. They have been so convincing that I believed for a while, in their colour-blind stance, that every staff would be treated equally based on merits and discrimination of any sort would not be tolerated. Silly me, I let my guard down, forgot my place, crossed the line they had drawn for me and opened my mouth to protest. In the end, I was smacked hard in the face for my perceived insolence and audacity. Sharing my episode of suicide attempt here is not to elicit sympathy votes and white saviourhood. Talking about the cost of racism is, however, an act of political resistance. What often accompanies racism is soul-crashing loneliness, self-gaslighting, self-blame and utter despair. It took me a while to begin the recovery from the suicide attempt, complex post-traumatic stress disorder, major depression and anxiety disorder. Probably akin to many writers who write about their trauma, after picking up our tattered and torn bodies, we summon our energies and souls to write. To write is to understand our lived experiences, expunge the toxicities out of our systems, fight back using our knowledges and politics, connect with other beautiful souls and worlds out there and hope that the nourishment we get from the learning, listening and writing process will ease the acute sense of alienation and hopelessness a little.

When I finally got back on my feet again, I started having a nagging suspicion that there must be other migrant women of colour employees within the Australian Academy out there with troubles similar to mine. They too could have been deemed as troublesome, insolent and ungrateful Asian women and were shouting silently in their pain and yearning inwardly to share their stories. I did not think I was alone in being bullied to silence and debilitation. In moments of solidarity, darkness and despair, I always find the words of women of colour, queer feminist greats the best therapy and compass. Audre Lorde's (2019) words spoke loudly:

> And where the words of women are crying to be heard, we must each of us recognise our responsibility to seek those words out, to read them and share them and examine them in their pertinence to our lives. (2019: 32)

Heeding Lorde's (2019) advice, I connected with forty other Asian migrant women employees in the academy. That began our collective storytelling connections. We bonded over our frustration, anguish and pain from the daily grind of racialization, discipline, invisibilization, reductive assumptions and overall dehumanization. Listening to the women's stories, I could not help but feel incredibly validated, supported and moved by their honesty, sincerity and solidarity. Their stories bore striking resemblances to mine and certainly helped dispel the intrusive self-gaslighting, self-blaming and self-bashing thoughts in my head. Their stories were enough to assure me that I was not oversensitive, overthinking and overreacting in the face of encounters with racial violence at the white colonial institution. I know that this archiving exercise of the Asian migrant women's stories has only touched the tip of the iceberg. There are certainly many other similar stories of racialization and racism against Asian migrant women employees in Australian universities waiting to be excavated, considered and documented.

I am telling our stories here not to create binary signposts of victimization versus agency or vulnerability versus resilience. Such restrictive and constrictive discourses demand minoritized subjects to be either victims who require saving and ignite white benevolence or agents who work to showcase their qualifications in deserving recognition not just from the dominator but also from well-meaning activists, scholars and community workers. Neither the victim that requires rescuing and deserves their voice to be heard nor the agent who must be celebrated for their resilience and strength will do anything to topple the dominator, change the rules of the game controlled by the master and inspire different ways of organizing social relations and systems for more sustainable and just existence. Worse, both victim and agency discourses only increase dopamine dosage for the white master, oppressor and saviour. The challenge then is how we may bring awareness of hidden stories of racial violence against the 'ornamental' Asian migrant woman subjects in the Australian Academy without falling into the trap of such victim–agent binary discourses and activating the unwelcome knee jerked impulses and obsessive-compulsive disorder of white powers to 'include' minoritized subjects, 'stand up for them' and 'give them a voice'. How can we explain that the problem to be fixed is not the women of colour themselves and certainly not their confidence level, leadership qualities and agency? How can we bring attention to the real roots of the problem without immediately activating repulsive whitewashing smokescreens such as multiculturalism, Equity, Diversity and Inclusion programmes, identity representation parades and other deflecting tactics?

The goal here is to join long-established, collective utterances and protests by race-critical, feminist and queer scholar-activists against oppressive structures that are always already set out to dominate and subjugate non-white subjects in the white, colonial academy. In line with the anti-coloniality, anti-capitalism and anti-racism greats' past and ongoing efforts, the project shows how oppressive racial capitalist, colonial workplaces and cultures not only affect distribution of life chances and successes but also shape micro-relations and interactions, which in turn strengthens existing unequal power structures and maintains status quo of white supremacy and colour-blindness. Through Asian migrant women university employees' stories, this chapter heightens awareness of the various modes of racism and coloniality in the Australian academy. Akin to Asian Americans embroiled in the model minority myth (Eng & Han 2018), Asian communities in Australia are commonly perceived as people who are compliant, successful, wealthy, well-adjusted, self-sufficient and good citizens and therefore exempt from racism and ill-treatment and do not need affirmative efforts and support. The book brings to readers' attention the racism and related forms of discrimination they encounter which are often disregarded or reduced due to their common portrayal of exemplary and hardworking migrants. It also brings to the forefront the historical, global, transnational and local structures of dominance that result in our shared predicaments even though we are affected differently, unevenly and unequally.

Our collective stories will add to the rich archives of stories of Asian migrant women who have come before us and travelled across lands to survive, live, connect, plough, grow and harvest. Readers may find our stories relatable and feel validated when our stories strike a chord with their personal experiences. Some may, however, feel that there is nothing new about our stories, and they have heard these stories before, sadly. I stress that the repeated telling of our stories is a political act and an important feminist work. Our stories must be told loudly even if they have been told before. Our stories must be told repeatedly as long as we need to for redress and revolution to take place. We need to keep bearing witness collectively of each other's stories, come together to give testimonies and, in the words of one respondent, 'tell racism like it fucking is' – cut-throat, brutally honest, reproaching with no holds-back. Our collective articulation of experiences, insights and strategies contributes to the global arsenal of anti-colonial and anti-racial capitalist feminist knowledges emerging out of our theories, philosophies and practices. Several respondents expressed deep appreciation of the opportunity to tell their stories:

> I wanted to start by thanking you for doing this research because this is not an easy topic. And I can't imagine what you're hearing. And the effect of this. So thank you for that.

Some lamented over the social isolation they experienced while facing racism in their everyday life and the lack of opportunity and safe space to share their encounters with racism in Australian universities:

> I'm really appreciative of you listening to my story. Cause I've been really isolated. Yeah, I want someone to listen to my story. I was really frustrated. I feel so indebted, feel so grateful, that you're willing to.

Another respondent echoed the same sentiment:

> You are the first one that I opened my heart to confide in you and share. I do not dare to share this with other colleagues. The university is so small. You share with one and in five minutes, words will spread to the other end.

Some women felt that racism faced by migrant women of colour has not been given recognition and importance in the broader discussion on racism in Australian society and academy. They protested about their employer and the broader industry being more invested in posturing their curated and whitened appreciation of Indigenous cultures and histories than addressing multiple migrant communities' marginalized experiences in Australia's colonial and race-making projects.

One common sentiment among respondents is that racism isolates them, makes them doubt and gaslight themselves if they have been imagining the violence or are too sensitive and overreacting and instils a sense of guilt for complaining and not displaying gratitude for their privileges. Some respondents indicated that their partnership in this project helped heal self-gaslighting:

> When I found out that you were doing this, I was really excited and glad that I wasn't the only one who thinks like that. I am really glad to be part of this.

Another respondent also said that sharing their stories spoke back to the intrusive voices of self-blame and self-doubt:

> I've been talking to myself. Am I too much? It's ruining emotions and people's lives … The worst is when you are facing racism or you are disrespected, and you don't know what to do or how to deal with it, or how to stop others from disrespecting you … This project is much valuable for me.

The women's collaboration in this collective archiving of stories project is significant in bearing witness to and documenting slow deaths induced by life-snubbing systems and practices of colonial, imperialist, racial capitalist and neoliberal machinery. One respondent expressed how existing institutional mechanisms were futile in making real change and believed this project featuring the women's first-hand accounts of being body slammed brutally and relentlessly by racism would not only bring them a sense of validation but also affirm many survivors out there:

> Your research is what I really appreciate, it is something that is gonna highlight the issues and getting the stories about people who face problems like me … It is more than just trying to make an official

complaint or investigation and it's not going to go anywhere … They gonna give them training about how to speak to us and nothing is going to come out of it … What you are doing is really, really, really helpful, even though I'm crying now, but hopefully in the future, if someone else is going through the same as me, they know that they are not alone … If someone is going through the same, they are not imagining it … There are other people that are going through the same and they need to know they are not crazy or imagining things … so hopefully this project raises awareness, and if you need me in anything, I can help out with anything, I'm happy to participate in anything. It's voluntary from my end. This is totally from me towards the cause. I am totally with you if you need me for any of that. People are suffering. We need to change.

Audre Lorde (2019) urges, 'for it is not difference which immobilises us, but silence. And there are so many silences to be broken' (2019: 33). We can never speak enough about the Asian immigrant women's stories of coming up against the racial-capitalist weaponry grinding them down to dust every day through being racialized by and co-opted into race-making projects. Too many stories must be told, heard and written about how the women are continually forced to capacitate themselves to fulfil racialized roles and expectations and, as a result, suffer from slow debilitation while at the same time, reap material benefits. The forty women and I came together to speak against the myths that have been imposed on us, speak about the contradictory clash of privileges and injuries and speak up about the ways in which we fight to break free of the constrictions. Our stories hope to open up an investigation and contribute a way of thinking, interpreting and recording of Asian migrant women's racialized experiences in Australian Academy and wider settler-colonial Australian society.

Myth of 'non-white, non-Indigenous, not racialized'

There's no sense that there are others of us who are not white, not indigenous … no one actually asks for our experiences … It is very important to know about Indigenous cultures and their history. But what about the other people who migrated here long, long ago …

Here, we do a lot of work on righting the wrongs with First Nations peoples and we should because we are not even doing enough … I think we miss that other group because they go, oh well, they're just culturally diverse others, so we just clump them all in one group.

Not-white, not-Indigenous, not anything is what this and many other Asian migrant women in the project described to relate their profound sense of insignificance and disregard despite toiling hard, displaying exemplary work ethics and performing more service and housework than their white colleagues. As I reflected upon the respondents' narratives, Cathy Park Hong's description of the Asian condition in the United States came to mind. Hong (2020) wrote,

> Asians lack presence. Asians take up apologetic space. We don't even have enough presence to be considered real minorities. We're not racial enough to be token… (2020: 7)

> … not white enough nor not black enough; distrusted by African Americans, ignored by the whites, unless we're being used by whites to keep the black man down. We are the carpenter ants of the service industry, the apparatchiks of the corporate world. We are math-crunching middle managers who keep the corporate wheels greased but who never get promoted since we don't have the right 'face' for leadership. (2020: 9)

Not white enough to be regarded as equal, intelligible and English-speaking but yet not Black enough to be considered as 'real minorities' deserving of white sympathy and benevolence is the common Asian condition the women of this project described as well. The women respondents spoke about their aesthetic, translucent and almost ghostly existence in Australian society and academy. What the myth of 'not white, not black' does to Asian migrant women is that their racialization is invisible, unseen and disregarded. They are not easily considered as targets and producers of racism as if the world is black and white with white people being the oppressor and Indigenous Black people being the oppressed, hence leaving no imagination of non-white, non-Black peoples' predicaments and implications in ongoing white race making projects. By discussing the women's complaints about their ornamental existence, it is not to argue for their visibility and recognition since such debates often degenerate into a portrayal of victimhood and immediate activation of white benevolent rescue missions. Far from playing into and encouraging the white powers' game where minoritized subjects fight among themselves to be 'included' and receive whatever crumbs they have been allowed to have, I am interested in the question of how this Asian condition came about.

To understand how Asian migrant women employees in Australian universities are caught up in a contemporary racialized existence and fraught relationships with white settler-majority, Indigenous peoples and other non-white immigrant-settlers, we need to go all the way back to examine the colonial context that laid the foundation of racialized power systems at their workplace in Australian settler-colonial society. During the British colonial rule, the always unstable colonial economic structure was heavily reliant on the constant flow of labour and innovation of labour extraction to ensure that labour supply was superfluous in generating and increasing profits. Like in North America, the early mass importation and settlement of Chinese, Indian and other groups of Asian labourers in settler-colonial Australia are not accidental. Across settler-colonial countries, the expansion of British empire saw the 'explicitly racialised ... decision to experiment with a different form of labour', and the strategy was to import a 'newly, and differently "raced" Chinese labour as a solution to both the colonial need to suppress Black slave rebellion and the capitalist desire to expand production' (Lowe 2015: 23). The importation of Asian coolies from China, India and other parts of the region kick-started the modern form of racial governmentality where the Asian coolie became a 'figure' symbolizing the transition of enslaved labour to 'free' labour and embracement of enlightenment and civility (Lowe 2015). The imported Asian migrant labour is therefore always already set up to be supplementary in the colonial labour structure – as an add on to

Indigenous and African slave labour, a replacement of the latter when slavery was abolished and as a filler when white convict labour supply ran low (Lowe 2015).

> In Australia, the Chinese replaced convict labour; the introduction of Chinese labour into New South Wales was not precipitated by the end of African slavery as it as in the Americas, but generated by the shortage of another form of unfree labour, that of prisoners in penal settlements in which over half of the population had arrived as convicts, yet whose numbers by 1851 had dwindled to fewer than 15 percent. (Lowe 2015: 27–8)

This colonial division of labour sets the scene of treating Asian immigrant labour as always interchangeable, replaceable, dispensable, commodified and disposable.

The emphasis of historical colonial context is key in explaining the continuing treatment of Asian immigrant labour according to the same racial capitalist logic to respond to changing and unstable demands of the economy in contemporary white settler-colonial societies. This importation, mobilization and hierarchical division of racialized labour also saw to the deployment of Asian labour force as an intermediary between Indigenous slaves and white British colonial settlers and accomplice of British colonial expansion projects to dispossess, kill, destroy and debilitate Indigenous peoples (Lowe 2015). What this hierarchical, racialized labour structure engineered by British colonialists did is anxiety-inducing on a few levels. It laid the foundation of Indigenous peoples' understandable and rightful anxieties, scepticisms and suspicions towards Asian immigrants since the latter were brought in without consulting and seeking permission from the Indigenous communities to collude with, enrich and empower the colonialists at their expense. Indigenous scholar Aileen Moreton-Robinson (2020b) critiqued non-white migrant-settlers as enablers of colonial possession whose 'sense of belonging is tied to the fiction of Terra Nullius and the logic of capital' and 'sanctioned by the law that enabled dispossession' of Indigenous peoples (Moreton-Robinson

2020b: 26). Even as non-white immigrants are 'differently positioned in relation to British imperialism', they nevertheless enter 'a colonising relationship between themselves and Indigenous peoples' (Moreton-Robinson 2020b: 29). Moreton-Robinson (2020b) also reminded that the colonialists did not go home and therefore Australia remains a colonizing-settler society where Indigenous peoples continue to be dispossessed by non-Indigenous peoples including white and non-white immigrant-settlers. The divide-and-rule colonial administrations also ensured that the colonized and subjugated populations did not interact and form alliances and intimacies (Lowe 2015) and set the conditions for their relationships to be estranged, strained, guarded and distant. Such anxieties in their relationships persist in contemporary white settler-colonial societies. What the colonial assignment of intermediary and supplementary role to Asian migrant labour also did is that it set Asian immigrant-settlers up as transient economic migrants perceived to be free as opposed to enslaved natives to exchange their labour for material gains. It not only placed them in an ambiguous, liminal, differentiated intermediary position distrusted by local Indigenous peoples but also set them up in survival and competition mode dispossessing Indigenous peoples and pitting against other immigrant-settlers to overcome exploitative work conditions, assimilate and accumulate wealth for a better life for themselves and families.

Supplementing the workforce of enslaved Indigenous, Asian indentured and white convict labourers, Chinese and Indian immigrant women were imported to work as domestic helpers in colonial households for the reproduction of European colonial bourgeois marriage and family (Haskins 2021; Lowrie 2021). Under the colonial division of labour, the Asian migrant woman is used to act as an intermediary between the colonialist and Indigenous enslaved, co-opted to act on behalf of the colonial master to discipline the Indigenous and other indentured labourers into assimilation and submission and, consequently, reaping material gains for survival and class mobility through earning the tolerance of their colonial master. One prominent myth imposed on the Asian migrant woman by the colonialists is the instrumental fantasy of 'Chinese women's sexuality resembling the "civility" of European marriage and family, in an implicit contrast to the sexualised representations of female African and African-descendant peoples' (Lowe 2015: 33). Co-opted into the colonial household as domestic helper, the women were used to reproduce European colonial, bourgeois households, learn civility of European women, marriage and family, reproduce colonial meanings and practices of intimacy in their own Asian migrant household and regulate other subjugated peoples to resemble European civility. Asian women were expected to model after the pristine, demure and desexualized European woman.

These supplementary, instrumental and intermediary roles persist till today; for example, Asian migrant women in the Australian academy continue to be used to reproduce civility of Eurocentric knowledge systems in every function of the academy. Women of colour are taught to model after the white civil woman with her dominant colour-blind gender and sexuality norms especially in the university's gender equity and women's leadership space. They are groomed to always be like the white woman – lean in, be confident, be as good as the white man, be pristine and respectful, do it all and the list goes on. The women and I are therefore not imagining the racialized myths imposed on us and the resulting racial suspicions, anxieties and instabilities we encounter in our everyday existence and interactions in the settler-colonial society.

In many ways, the Asian migrant woman in the Australian academy is still performing a large portion of domestic service and housework. While it has been widely observed that women employees carry a larger pastoral care and administrative load in the university compared to their men counterparts, it is worthwhile considering the even greater load women of colour employees must bear. Some respondents related that they have been performing more care work for students of colour who would feel more comfortable turning to them instead of white faculty for support. A first-generation migrant, mid-career respondent in her thirties related how she indeed felt like a domestic servant picking up pastoral care work while her white colleagues got to discuss academic research with students:

Some of the students see Asian women as more subservient and more passive. It doesn't matter about my seniority whether I was a casual tutor, first year of my PhD, or senior professor. They treat me in a way that make me pause and wonder, 'Do you see me as your servant?' I've had students say to me, 'Your assignment is due the same time as my assignment with Dr Steve White Man, and so could I get an extension for your subject?' And I said, 'Oh, did you ask Dr White Man for an extension to his subject?' The student replied, 'Oh no, he's too busy, I don't want to bother him'. So it's just like things like that. Little small things … .I've had students, including students of color who might still be engaged in that white worship … they would go to the white male professor to talk about theory, paper ideas and writing, and then they would come to me if they wanted a shoulder to cry on because they were stressed. I felt like I was doing disproportionate amount of emotional labor. There was some kind of racial, gender dimension to that labor division.

Another respondent in her thirties, a second-generation descendant of a refugee family, put it poignantly, 'I'm the shift in the kitchen in the back and the white woman's the front of house at the restaurant and her responsibility as the front of house is to speak to the diners and stuff like that while I work at the back in the kitchen.' Like the Asian immigrant women domestic helpers imported to reproduce European colonial bourgeois marriage and family, the Asian migrant women workers in contemporary Australian academy play a supplementary but nevertheless significant role to reproduce the colonial institution and accentuate its white powers. The colonial legacy of racialized division of labour pre-determines Asian migrant women's supplementary, accessory, nevertheless functional role in supporting the reproduction of the white heteropatriarchal institution. Seldom allowed to take centre stage, they play an important supporting act in the white academy's racializing projects. Mentioned earlier in the book, Anne Anlin Cheng (2019) highlights that while the yellow woman may appear insignificant in her ornamental position, she in fact is made to play an important role in the race-making of modern white man personhood. Her ornamental Asiatic femininity, like dehumanized black enslaved body, is constructed to accentuate the superiority of white humanity. In this project, the yellow womanhood does not refer to the Oriental woman; rather it refers to the ornamental personhood and its proximity to white racial capitalist advancements and distance from dispossession and enslavement.

The narratives of this study's respondents unfortunately present excessive evidence of how they have been racialized, sexualized and ornamentalized and how their exoticization and infantization conscript and implicate them in white race-making. One respondent who arrived in Australia in 1980s for her PhD studies narrated the racialization and exoticization of Asian women she experienced:

> When I first came here, I was seen as exotic … the racism was more about my accent and being seen as exotic … they look at me and go, my clothes are so nice … It wasn't the abusive form of racism but more like seeing me as exotic.

Whether white colleagues are conscious about their acts of racialization of non-white people, this exoticization of non-white people nevertheless works to remind non-white people that they are primitive and not civilized like modern white people. This is not just racism and white ignorance of the past. Up till recently, a respondent in her forties, who moved to Australia with her family when she was nine years old, received such demeaning comments from white colleagues stemming from their own racial superiority:

> I moved from a massive city … white people didn't really understand what my home country was like. I still remember being asked whether I lived in a tree. You know, I lived in a city that has a population size bigger than this entire country and you asked me if I lived in a tree, and then, of course, there were the questions of how long did it take me to learn how to speak English, etc. Well, actually, I only ever speak English, and we speak better English than you do here.

This everyday exoticization of Asian migrant women is significant in white race-making, where white superiority is strengthened and racial hierarchy kept intact. The entrapment of Oriental and exotic frames brings about unwanted, at times repulsive, sexual-racial harassment and advances displaying white patriarchal power. Several women in the study related encounters at meetings and conferences where white male colleagues were more interested to comment about their skin colour, body, appearance and dressing than work and expertise. One horrifying account reads like this:

> He just happened to be sitting in front of me at the conference dinner table. He was a middle-aged white man from an European background. He was fascinated about how great my country is. When the dinner was over, he came forward and hugged me. I felt really uncomfortable because he pressed me, and sniffed me, and he said, 'that feels so good'. And I was like oh, my God, this is so gross! I don't want to see this person anymore … When the break started and he had gone to Europe somewhere, he didn't even know me, didn't have my email address but he had found my email address and started sending me really creepy emails about how he is in Europe right now, and he likes this museum and how I remind him of these oriental gardens, and he wanted to see if I'm available for a dinner when he comes back.

Horrified, I listened to another respondent, a first-generation migrant in a senior position, relate a more belligerent encounter of sexual-racial transgression at an academic conference when the aggressor displayed his white patriarchal entitlement to her being and violent misogyny in the face of rejection:

> I had one instance where, after a conference, one of these white men who I rejected showed up at my accommodation and said he was there … He was screaming at me because I turned him down, and while our conversations were initially cordial, he started screaming things like, 'Oh, your Asian slut. You're probably not very good anyway' … It was very ugly. He's an established academic and I know the students he teaches. I still had to see him at other conferences following the event.

Asian immigrant women trapped in this aesthetic Asiatic feminine frame constructed for them by white powers regularly face such racialized and sexualized harassment and threats to their safety at the workplace.

To begin with, the respondents' workplace is predominately a colonial institution that was first and foremost created for the propagation of Western imperialism and supremacy of Eurocentric civilizations, world views and knowledge systems and continues to systematically regard as the inherited colonial education systems as default and superior. It is therefore no surprise that the respondents would describe their workplace as firmly rooted in white, heteropatriarchal systems and cultures. In recent years, their workplace has begun to signal diversity, decolonization and indigenization with a range of cultural competence initiatives, but some respondents reckoned that such cultural celebrations were more of a cosmetic, aesthetic and demonstrative posture of 'inclusion and diversity' rather than a genuine political will to redistribute power, privileges and resources in concrete ways. The women's supplementary value in the academy's corporate diversity and inclusion investments is significant though for the institution's white race-making projects. The women I spoke with described extensively many examples of how they have been ornamentalized in the classroom, research spaces and professional settings.

Frequently, even before the women open their mouths to speak, they have to deal with the assumption that they do not know how to speak English and, therefore, the consequent treatment of being immediately written off as less intelligent and capable requiring handholding and assistance from co-workers. The dominance of English language cannot be ignored here; English language has been globally used as a colonial tool to rank humanity, 'civilize' colonized populations and enhance contemporary racial capitalist projects. A glaring example is the global International English Language Testing System industry employed by English-speaking wealthier countries like the United States, UK, Canada, Australia and New Zealand to milk capital from desperate and aspiring immigration applicants from less wealthy, mostly formerly colonized, countries in the Global South. The women in the project complained how they are commonly assumed to not understand and speak English because they are not white; they are in turn perceived as unintelligent because they are assumed to not know how to speak

English. Consistent to colonial racialization system, skin colour and language proficiency continue to be used to evaluate and rank humanity at the women's workplace in modern Australian academy. Conversely, a white person, even before opening their mouth to speak, is assumed to speak English at a proficient level and thereby instantly taken in as intelligent and capable. Several respondents indicated that it was common for students to comment on their English language proficiency and ascent in official feedback on their teaching, online platforms or class discussions. Feedback like these are shamefully aplenty:

> In the student evaluations, I had one comment basically saying that she can't speak English;

> I don't understand her accent, she needs to speak better English;

> Not that she doesn't know how to explain shit. She can't speak English lmao;

> in the discussions, they raise questions about my English proficiency and said, 'I think you don't understand' … They are just questioning something and challenging me. They were hostile, disrespectful and arrogant. They also showed that I was not a native speaker and did not understand what I was saying … definitely they were racist against me.

Fellow academic and professional co-workers also often made references to the women's English language proficiency and, as usual, expressed surprise when they could speak good English:

> Some people at the conference would later say, 'You can speak English really well'. But I did my PhD in Australia. I have a masters, so why are you so surprised? People think that a non-white scholar cannot explain themselves as well, so we'll have to publish lots of books, articles just to let them see that, yes, we know the stuff we are talking about even if you don't feel that we can.

Like this respondent, a few others also complained how white colleagues would speak slowly and loudly believing that they were doing their non-white colleague a favour since they assumed by virtue of their skin colour, their non-white colleague did not understand English:

She started to speak to me quite slowly and clearly. At first, I gave the benefit of doubts and thought maybe she thinks I don't know how to speak English. I was telling her about how I thought I speak good English but when I come to Australia, the idioms are quite interesting and different. The woman looked at me and asked, 'And do you speak English now?' I was quite taken aback. I did not mean I did not understand English, just think the expressions are different. I mean I expect racism when I come here but still when it happened, I was taken aback. Then one woman turned around and spoke very slowly, 'Do … you … know …' I mean I was already speaking in English for half an hour and you still think I don't know how to speak and understand English. People just expect that you don't know how to speak English because of the colour of your skin. You know what it is like … People just decide on their own and speak very loudly and slowly to you.

By slowing down in their speech, white colleagues might believe that they were being culturally sensitive and considerate, but this respondent protested that the condescending act only reinforced whiteness, white people's racial superiority, dominance of English language and subordination of non-white people:

I also feel that I am pitied. They think they have to slow down for me. They think they have to let me speak slowly. People think they are showing cultural sensitivity and high cultural awareness. But to me, such racism is the same. It is tokenistic. I just want to be treated equally and be respected.

Another respondent who has lived in Australia and worked as an academic for two decades related how she had been made to repeat herself when conversing with white colleagues as if they did not understand what she was saying:

Sometimes when I talk to my white colleagues, I find myself having to repeat everything I have to say. They somehow chose not to understand my accent. I don't think I have an accent that is so difficult to understand. I also don't think my choice of words and expressions are so bad that they don't understand what I am saying. It is these kinds of things. People don't remember my face, my name, don't understand what I am saying and make me repeat things.

This respondent, a first-generation migrant in her late forties who has lived in English-speaking countries for more than two decades, explained clearly the extra amount of labour she found herself having to put in to deal with this specific everyday manifestation of racism:

The white women administrative staff didn't seem to be able to understand me. Apparently I didn't speak English. I had to ask for everything three or four times, just had to work really hard to get the smallest amount of support or help … a bit of that was quite sad and depressing, and that just gone on, that just never stopped. And when I've raised it with managers, I've been told not to be thin skinned, or that I'm imagining things.

As Toni Morrison (1975) said, 'the very serious function of racism … is distraction. It keeps you from doing your work. It keeps you explaining, over and over again, your reason for being.'

What is also prominent in the women's narratives on everyday racialization and ornamentalization is their white colleagues' profound lack of interest in knowing people of colour co-workers, learning their names, finding out about their lives and even remembering who they are after interacting with them for a reasonable amount of time. One first-generation migrant respondent in her forties and at a senior academic career stage shared her unpleasant encounter with a white man colleague:

I have many experiences of my white colleagues not remembering who I am despite that I have spent time with them. For example, I met a white male academic staff member on a business trip as part of the university delegation. We stayed at the same hotel. We spent an intensive period of four days together. He asked me about the local market. I brought him there. We have gone to the market together for one day, sat through meals for four days and attended conference together. So it wasn't just nodding head and hello kind of interaction … But when we met again, he had no idea who I was. Maybe I just wasn't so memorable. Maybe because I am a non-Caucasian female colleague who has nothing to do with him on a daily basis so he does not remember me. This has happened many times. It is not just one incident.

These experiences of being disregarded by white colleagues are unfortunately far too common as testified by this other respondent who expressed difficulty in calling out causal, relational racism in the form of being iced out and ignored:

> My team is very white. I am the only Asian person. There is one team member who will not have eye contact with me throughout the team meetings. It is a feeling of being made feel unimportant, disregarded, disrespected. I feel that I did not get equal respect. I ask myself am I too sensitive? Am I imagining things? Am I overthinking? This kind of subtle, relational racism is so hard to call out. It is not so overt and direct that you can call out. These people are normally very sensitive to others and so much talk about inclusiveness but behaviour proves otherwise.

Some respondents also complained about being treated as if their presence was decorative and did not matter in social settings with white co-workers as opposed to being taken seriously when interacting with people of colour colleagues:

> A lot of white colleagues are just really comfortable to talk out loud, and there's no opportunity for me to say anything … I only noticed this difference after I collaborated with a small team of all people of colour researchers. I was actually able to speak for extended periods of time in meetings – it felt so different because they wanted to hear what I had to say.

The women's racialization also manifests in ways where their differences are ignored. There are many accounts of how white colleagues confuse them with another Asian woman colleague. An ethnic Chinese respondent from a Southeast East Asian country complained about being mistaken as another East Asian, ethnic Chinese colleague.

A South Korean respondent was asked to speak about Singapore and had to protest, 'I am not even Singaporean, I am Korean.' A South Asian woman respondent lamented over the lack of interest among her white colleagues to find out if she was from India, Bangladesh, Pakistan, Fiji or another country:

> Even after three to four years of working here, people confuse my name with another brown woman's, and that other brown woman colleague was called my name … they think you are all from the same place, just another brown person … once I was told that I am very lucky to have brown skin because I won't get skin cancer.

As part of the overall racialization and ornamentalization of Asian migrant women, being infantilized is an everyday predicament the women in the sample experienced at the workplace. The infantilization could sometimes be displayed through physical gestures. It was hard to listen to this respondent's account:

> There's a kind of belittling people like me in the sector. I've had instances where senior female white professors have tapped me on the head. Clearly, because they don't see you as someone who could possibly be in the same space as them.

Another first-generation migrant respondent in her thirties, though more qualified in her research expertise and teaching experience than her white man teaching co-worker, shared this common experience of infantilization in the classroom:

> Last year I was teaching a unit and I was paired with the male white colleague … I am a PhD in that area, and my white male colleague was just starting his PhD. I was the one who has taught for five consecutive years, and he just started teaching the unit. Whenever we were having class discussions, there are a group of male students in the classroom who would only respond to my white male colleague, completely overlooking me. My colleague, who would challenge me in front of the students. I don't think this would be an issue that white colleagues would be experiencing.

Several respondents related many occurrences where students and colleagues would mistake them for students, research assistants or more junior-ranked professional staff. A respondent in her late thirties who has established a successful academic career related her experience as an invited speaker at conferences:

> What usually happens is when I rock up to the podium, people think I am the research assistant there to help prepare the speaker's slides before she comes. They think I'm there to put water on the podium before she arrives. And it's only when I introduce myself that people realize who I am. I don't think a man who is in his 30s or a white woman in her 30s will get this. It's not an age thing. Honestly, it's the infantilising of my expertise and my status because of my race and my visual make up.

I have discussed earlier that the historical colonial division of labour set Asian migrant women up as supplementary and intermediary for the reproduction of colonial bourgeois institutions and white supremacy. As Alana Lentin (2020) explains, race is fundamentally a 'technology for the management of human difference, the main goal of which is the production, reproduction and maintenance of white supremacy on both a local and planetary scale' (2020: 5). In the contemporary context of Australian academy, the women's accounts reveal how they were repeatedly pigeonholed in specific supplementary work functions and research areas designated to them mainly for white race-making projects. As if to fulfil white fantasies of the ornamental roles Asian migrant women are supposed to play, they are assigned with culture-specific work to display cultural diversity and, in turn, accentuate whiteness. Even when it is not their research and work areas, they are typecast to be an expert of their cultural and language backgrounds and either only permitted to work in assigned culture and language specific areas or tasked to carry the representation load. For example, one respondent protested that she was trained in English literature but found herself being gradually directed to do Chinese or China-related work over the course of her career because she is ethnic Chinese. Or another respondent though trained in social sciences could only find language teaching work in the university if she wanted to be employed. An early career researcher respondent shared this account of racialized allocation of work where she was pressured by senior white colleagues to speak about a social issue she has researching on in relation to her cultural background, hence further reinforcing racial stereotypes of her cultural community:

> I wanted to present certain things based on my research at the conference but I just didn't get the opportunity because when they saw me and knew a bit about my background, they just assumed that I would only be able to talk about one aspect of the work pertaining to culturally and linguistically diverse communities ... they said you are from that community and that's what you should talk about ... I just feel that that's where you end up, you are just that token representative ... it's that bias that's that keeps coming up because when you were hired, you were not hired specifically to advise on CALD communities, but yet when you started working you found yourself being boxed in that way ... even that to me is a different form of kind of racism ... it's white privilege ... they feel like they're doing this for inclusivity and diversity whereas that is not the case, it's more singling you out and boxing you in ... when we are being boxed this way, we have to carry many things ... we have to worry about how we are portraying to the white Australians ... how we are betraying our community to the white Australian people ... how we are also portraying our community to our own community people.

Such job delegations and representation load subordinate the women to the white powers' control, restrict their mobility within the white institution, specify the perimeters they are allowed to roam and make them an accessory in white race-making projects. All this evidence points to the ways in which racialization of Asian immigrant women employees in the Australian academy fulfil white fantasies of them as ornamental, supplementary and intermediary.

   Fire Dragon Feminism

Myth of 'well-poised, mobile and achieving migrant women'

'What does it mean to survive as someone too aestheticised to suffer injury but so aestheticised that she invites injury?', asks Cheng (2019: xi). Propped up like a porcelain vase, the Asian woman is portrayed as delicate, exotic and decorative. Enshrined in her aestheticism, the Asian migrant woman appears to be polished and untainted. So aesthetic that the Asian immigrant woman invites injury but yet so aesthetic that her racialization and racial injuries are not always obvious, noticed and believed. Building on the earlier section on the racialization and ornamentalization of Asian migrant women in white settler-colonial societies, this section continues to explore the myths imposed on the women and extends the discussion on their oftentimes unnoticed and disbelieved racial injuries. I am mindful that by writing about their disenfranchisement, it may be read as recuperative platforming victimhood and, consequently, triggering the unwanted, overactive white saviourhood condition. I therefore would like to caution again that the objective here is to foreground the historical and contemporary structures and conditions that shape Asian migrant women's decorative, nevertheless instrumental, racialized relations in white racial capitalist projects such as the Australian academy. Echoing Cheng's (2019) ornamentalism project's objective, this section exposes the disparaging conditions that produce extensive aestheticization and violence of unnoticed Asiatic femininity instrumental in white race-making and the resulting 'wounds that the indifferent public, … the well-intentioned liberal, and sometimes our loved ones tell us are longer wounds' (2019: xiii).

Being imposed with the myth of a well-poised, striving and successful migrant citizen means that the women and I (un)consciously and (un)knowingly work inwardly and outwardly to meet its imagined and real-life expectations. As basic as physical appearance, we make alterations to look more 'Western, white and modern' so that white people would find us attractive, intelligible, civilized, proper or a bit more like them is a common self-grooming, self-help and personal development chore my respondents and I have to perform. A first-generation migrant respondent in her late thirties and at an early career stage shared how she changed her dressing style so as to get her white colleagues to talk to her:

> You know how over here, growing up, you want to dress like your friends to fit in but you cannot fit in. Then you dress your own style, dye your hair and wear what you want, suddenly you fit in. It is like not fitting in to fit in. It's like that in the academy. When I dress black jeans, proper shirt and leather shoes, it is okay in my home country, considered formal. But if I dress like that it, people think you are a boring Asian and nobody wants to talk to you, you feel ostracised … then one day, I realise maybe I got to mix it up, mix up my dressing. Then this guy came up to me and said, 'Wow your slippers are very cool.' I then suddenly realise I have to mix up my dressings, appear not fit in to fit in. All these may seem very small things but it is actually very tiring. I think when I go to those school lunches now, people are less reluctant to talk to you. Because it is a new job, I need to fit in right?

We do this not just to improve our acceptance index at the white workplace, which in turn may open doors to career progression and class mobility, but also in hope that our sad efforts would reduce casual and relational racism we experience in our everyday work life. Another respondent shared how her students complained that her cultural dress and jewellery were making too much noise that it distracted them from learning, and she had to 'tone down' her Indian accessories to accommodate white students' preferred learning style and avoid further racialized treatments. At one point, I shaved one side of my head to show off a lightning-patterned undercut and would clip my hair up so that my white colleagues would see it. My desire to speak white and avoid everyday disrespect, condescension, infantilization and hostility ran so deep that I got myself two origami tattoos on visible parts of my arms. In an exaggerated attempt to differentiate myself from boring Asians that white people snub with contempt, I chose to inflict pain on and introduce ink into two prominent spots of my lower arm where white people could easily see my origami dragon and rabbit tattoos, make a mental note to themselves that I am modern just like them and strike up a conversation with me about my tattoos. Since I have learnt how to speak white, I know that I would appeal to white people if I am modern by their standards but, at the same time, dial up my Asian heritage in ways that appear exotic, mysterious and mystical but never confrontational and threatening to them. I chose Japanese origami style tattoos of my and my partner's Chinese horoscopes, and I make sure I roll up my sleeves and flap my tattooed arms in front of my white colleagues, students, neighbours and friends every time we interact. There is no playbook for this, but some of my respondents and I have learnt through trials and tribulations how to read and crack the code of speaking white. It is almost a craft we learn to acquire and improve on so that we are less of an opaque and non-consequential Asian woman, and white people would then be less reluctant to talk to us, as the respondent above put it. Our accounts bring to mind a poem, *What shall I wear to work today?* by Roanna Gonsalves, an award-winning author of *The permanent resident* (Gonsalves 2016), poet and academic born and grew up in Mumbai, India, and living and working in Australia since late 1990s:

What shall I wear to work today?

– Roanna Gonsalves
(first published in Joao-Roque Literary Journal, 2018,
reproduced here with permission)

A sari's drape is nothing like a suit.
A pin-striped jacket's cut is far more slick.
When glass and bamboo ceilings need the boot,
they say a trouser'd likely do the trick.
A buttoned blazer covers all the bases,
where ghagra, pallo, pleats might come undone.

A matching skirt and blouse'd take you places,
no midriff bare, distracting everyone.
My Mysore silk, my grandma's kanjeevaram,
my kasavu, ikat, darned old kantha fave,
they're all unsuited to the peak-hour scrum
of worsted wool, cashmere, and tweed so grave
> And yet, I'll do my sari's fall and bidding.
> I'll worship, wear this comfort, live, enfolding.

The crux of racism is exertion of power and control over minoritized subjects and their existence. The control could manifest in the forms of self-surveillance, self-censorship and self-capacitation to fulfil imposed racialized myths and roles as shown above in the ways which we alter our physical appearances and dressings to be white enough for white people to interact with us albeit condescendingly. It could also happen when external sources actively gatekeep borders of whiteness. The narratives of the women in this study show that they are not exactly the autonomous and mobile Asian migrant women with equitable access to physical, social and professional spaces. A prominent theme that emerged out of the women's stories is the restriction of mobility. The women in this study reported finding out the perimeters of enclosure they were permitted to move within and the manner and pace they must move in to avoid rousing white rage, insecurity and disapproval. It appeared to them that they would only be tolerated, accepted and, at times, noticed and given certain leadership roles if they demonstrated understanding of the borders of their allotted space and would stay within them. Sometimes, the restriction of mobility is physical. An early career, first-generation migrant respondent related a sickening experience of being told to leave the allocated office and move to another office because a white woman colleague sharing the workspace with her did not want her there:

University assigned me a room … it's shared room, so I started moving, and there was another person in that room … white woman and she said, 'You should not move here, it will be very crowded. Can you please move to the next door? I'm always working, I need some quiet time, you can move to next room.' I said, 'I can't move to next room if university does not allocate to me that room. If you don't want me to sit here, why don't you tell them to allocate me another room?' She said, 'No, you don't need to tell any staff. You just go to the next room.' I still moved there. There are days when I'm in the room, she would say similar things to me … On my train ride from a school event, I saw my head of school and told her everything. She was very upset, and she said, 'I don't know why people are this way. I just want them to be kind, to be helpful to help each other. This is so ungrateful!' She's white, she didn't use the word race or racism.

Her account reminded me of how my own Asian immigrant woman's body was scrutinized, made out of place and disallowed to appear in certain white spaces:

At the staff pantry where my partner and I were having lunch, a professional staff questioned our presence at the staff area, 'This is a staff pantry. Are you a student or a staff?' When I replied that we were part of the first year sociology teaching team, they were not convinced and continued their questioning: 'You are a staff? Who are you teaching with? What is the name of the subject coordinator?' All these exchanges were within the plain sight of other white colleagues using the pantry. I glanced at them hoping that one of them would put a stop to the professional staff's rude and condescending behaviour and let us eat in peace before our next class. No one did. Though the offender eventually walked away, their rudeness and arrogance were hard to stomach. Outraged and dejected, we lost our appetite for our lunch. (Quah 2020b: 206)

At times, the restriction of mobility is professional. In the area of career progression, a few respondents were told by their white managers not to apply for a particular job or promotion because their work unit required a woman of colour employee to do the diverse work the rest of the white team felt ill-equipped to carry out or that they were not qualified, suitable, ready and experienced enough for the position or promotion they wished to apply or that they were still young and could afford to wait for the next round of promotion. 'I feel that I would always be evaluated by different kinds of standards and expectations compared to my white colleagues', one respondent expressed. Some related their suspicions of contracts not being renewed or not being picked for jobs including internal governance roles because their white colleagues could not imagine them taking on certain roles and leadership positions typically occupied by white people. They spoke about the nagging worry of being labelled as only suitable to take up roles that involve international and diversity areas or nudged into research areas that are related to their nationality and cultural backgrounds or policed by white gatekeepers on what counts as the right type of research within disciplines they have been trained in and even the area studies they have been pressured to work on. One early career respondent in her late thirties put it eloquently about the boxes we have been put in and consequences for not staying within ascribed boxes:

> I've always felt there are boxes. I'm only welcome to stay within those boxes, and if I rise above those boxes, then I will be smashed. And it's not just by the patriarchal voice that comes from a white man. Sometimes it comes from another woman, sometimes it comes from another woman of color, sometimes it's another white woman … As a woman of color, I've constantly been forced into being hyper-vigilant thinking that racism is coming, strategising around it, keeping calm because if not I would be that hysterical woman. If I speak up about it, it was either that I would give myself into being saved or being smashed … a lot of white feminists were not comfortable with you writing too much, or talking too much.

Several respondents have also witnessed how gatekeepers aligned with the white institution closed in to censor, silence and punish those who dared to dissent. Those who went as far as lodging a formal complaint using the university's complaint management mechanism were gently but firmly persuaded that the incident in question was not racism but more about cultural differences or personality clashes. Official complaint handlers and line managers closed ranks to encourage the Asian woman complainer to educate herself instead of reading the situation as anything but racist. Often, the women encountered doubts and questions like, 'I wonder if this is racism', 'maybe it is not racism, just cultural differences', 'he does that to me too, not just you and women of colour', 'this is just matter of personality clash' and 'you are taking it personally, you're not being professional'. A respondent in her late thirties, who moved to Australia with her family as a young child, recounted her own experience in protesting against racism and observed that the non-white complainer would be told:

> You are the problem. You're the one being too sensitive. You're the one stirring the pot. You're the one accusing good white people of being racist, which is worse than being a racist. Accusing a good white person of being a racist is worse than having facing racism yourself.

It is as if 'a denial of the fact that this is how and where colonised bodies are made to dwell' (Ngo 2019: 248) will remove the deeply embedded racialized structures both white and non-white peoples have inherited and continue to inhabit. What could be observed here is the practice of 'white temporality' where white people could afford the historical luxury to display 'racialised forgetting', decide that coloniality is of the past, suspend present coloniality and urge colonized and racialized subjects to 'move on and get over it' (Ngo 2019: 249). This practice itself is a form of institutional racism where there is a systemic wilful amnesia of colonial histories and convenient ignorance of sustained colonial, racial capitalist structures maintaining dominance of white majority (Murji 2007; Better 2008; Ngo 2019; Quah 2020b). The denial of real and meaningful avenue to seek redress for racial injustices and injuries albeit the availability of official complaint mechanism is also evidence of institutional racism where the women's encounters with white gaslighting attest to. At times, the white gaslighting went a step further when white power holders framed their dismissal of racism as a form of protection. One respondent recounted how her good white woman manager supposedly steeped in decoloniality, feminism and

Asian studies presented her warning and threat in the form of advice when she complained about racism:

> She kept framing it like she was on my side, and I didn't know what to think about that. She said, you know you'd better be careful, because the university could sue you for defamation. She goes, 'Of course, we will protect you at all costs. But if you keep going around like this we may not be able to protect you' ... She was framing the whole thing like as I'm your mentor, I'm helping you. I'm warning you, and I'm going to protect you.

The gaslighting and associated institutional violence bounced off the women's complaints and undoubtedly broke them further. A disappointed and injured early career respondent in her thirties conceded defeat:

> To be honest with you, I am just gonna eat my experiences with racism and not talk about it with these people, because dealing with their white fragility, the defensiveness, you know, all the explaining that comes through, telling me that I'm wrong, we'd be a lot more hurt than just like acknowledging the fact that what they said was racist. You talk about the problem, but you end up being their care worker having to pat them on the shoulder and tell them, 'I'm so sorry that you had to go through this'. I'd rather invest my energy into something else.

Even when some of the respondents gave up fighting and instead embraced their aesthetic purpose, used it to their advantage and enrolled themselves into white racial capitalist projects as a diversity mascot, it was not quite an even playing field compared to their white counterparts. They objected to the extra length of time it took, additional number of hoops they must jump and many more detours they found themselves taking just to convince the white institution and power holders they have learnt the rules, are just as worthy as their white counterparts and deserving of a specific job or promotion. One respondent in her late forties who has recently secured a junior permanent employment position after being in the workforce for decades recounted:

> Of course, the institutional racism, I mean, it's so clear. Look how long it's taken me to get a frickin job, you know. I'm like an overachiever. I've done ten times more than the others … But we just have to take so long to convince them that we are half as good … in the institution, it's more whiteness as a norm not being taken seriously.

Another first-generation migrant respondent in her sixties, who moved to Australia in 1980s for studies and work, came to understand the limits of areas and pace she was allowed to move in and made necessary modifications to her movements, orientations and pathways to stay in the game:

> If I were born a white person, I am sure that I would be in a higher position … People put you in the box … They don't let you outside of the box … they don't acknowledge your abilities outside of the box … Because of the colour of your skin, there are things already pre-determined for you and not by you. I think it is great shame. It does affect you … But at the same time, I can also reconcile with the reality … I know I will have to adjust my expectations.

This respondent in her late forties, who migrated to Australia in early 2000s and currently held a professional role, also seemed resigned to the melded bamboo and glass ceilings she repeatedly banged her head on in her career track:

> I certainly did not move as fast as I could. When it comes to promotion, I am definitely not the first one they would consider. People will never consider me first. They will never see me first. They will never give me opportunity first.

These accounts only go to show that women of colour's mobility, whether it is moving across actual physical spaces or up the professional career ladder, is constricted and regulated. It is ultimately conditional upon approval of white gatekeepers of a colonial racial hierarchy that has already and continues to confine Asian women subjects as secondary and supplementary in white race-making enterprises.

What is also worth noting is that the restriction, constriction, surveillance and gaslighting are not only from external sources but also internalized. Not only do we alter our physical appearances and dressings to look white, but we also (un)consciously monitor our thoughts and behaviours to think, speak and do white. Some respondents related how they would 'unconsciously speak English faster, try to be fluent to present themselves better so as to find ways to improve the situation and avoid racism'. Self-alteration also comes in forms where the women perform the expected, allocated and sometimes remunerated role of Asian feminine ornament responsible for elevating whiteness. This sentiment by a respondent is familial:

> I know that a lot of the time I also had to play to that persona of being
> an Asian woman. I couldn't be too disruptive. I couldn't be too angry.
> I should be friendly. I had to be nice, and that takes a toll many years.

The key is learning our place determined by whiteness and engaging in self-modification to stay in allocated space for rewards or avoidance of punishment. The self-surveillance and self-evaluation spill over to the ways in which many respondents questioned their own appraisal of racialized treatments. Almost every respondent's sharing of racism experiences began with 'I don't know if this is racism'. It is almost as if the women I spoke with were unsure if they have been racialized and inflicted with racial injuries. Even at the point of the interview, they appeared to be self-gaslighting and wondered if they were indeed imagining things, overreacting and being too emotional, taking it personally and reading the situation wrong, as what they have been repeatedly told. A respondent in her forties on casual employment basis while pursuing a postgraduate degree related having a serious imposter syndrome even when it concerned her discernment of racist encounters:

> I did get a bit of imposter syndrome last week when I was sharing
> with a friend of mine, who is also a woman of color, and saying, 'I

don't know whether these experiences are racist enough to qualify me for taking up your time and talking about this' … I've just become so desensitized and just going with it. Did that person react like that? Or is that because they just having a bad day? Am I thinking like that because of the internalised racism? I don't know how to read it anymore.

Hong (2020) in her work on Asian Americans points out that while 'Asian Americans are fortunate not to live under hard surveillance', they 'live under a softer panopticon, so subtle that it's internalised, in that we monitor ourselves, which characterises our conditional existence' (2020: 202). If Asian migrant women have been set up to be ornamental and supplementary in white race-making, our external and internal orientations inevitably are towards white powers. Conscripted into whiteness, we check, alter and orientate ourselves (un)consciously to fulfil our ascribed decorative roles, outperform as model minorities and be as aesthetic as we could in order to be noticed, picked and rewarded. A respondent in her late sixties, who was an immigrant in 1980s and has worked in the Australian academy for more than three decades, explained the indescribable, omnipresent panopticon that propels her to look inwards, contort, amputate and morph into the space designated for her:

> Just that it's very subtle, you know. And I think that's part of the problem … It's a kind of atmosphere. It's an environment which discourages people of colour, and especially women of colour, from considering themselves as a whole, as a white person. And so you kind of self-regulate, self-censor.

This everyday conditional, ornamental existence weighs on our being and grinds us down. This respondent in her forties having lived and worked in Australia for two decades described her racialized paranoia and melancholia being in that unsettled, floating everyday reality:

> It made me really down at the time, like there was something wrong with me, I shouldn't raise issue, it's not an issue at all … How do we

tell the difference whether it has something to do with race? It makes us question ourselves. Is it really merit and that we are just not good enough or is it really race? Maybe we are not that confident, maybe we appear not confident, and that is attributed to us not being confident. It makes me wonder what's happening. Am I just not fitting in? Very often, these questions come to my mind.

Another respondent in her forties, a second-generation descendant of a refugee family, related the emotional toll of constantly questioning herself if she has been racially targeted:

It's a daily issue that I have to think about, thinking about was that racist or not? Am I over thinking it? Am I exaggerating in my mind? Did they mean it like that? That's exhausting. But it's a part of the everyday life of academia for me … It just feels like an additional job to be honest with it … We're just trying to do our work but this other side to our work that not many people see or understand takes an emotional toll, and then it's the resistance that adds another layer to our work. Supporting each other, women of colour is also another layer of work.

One other respondent, who grew up in Australia as a young child after her parents immigrated to Australia for better economic opportunities, shared that the racial self-surveillance, self-censorship and self-doubt affected her so deeply that she even curtailed her physical movement by choosing not to be on university's grounds:

I developed a strong sense of hypervigilance around 2020 and 2021. That's when I stopped going to campus because I don't want to walk on the campus and have to deal with someone being inadvertently racist or an inadvertent microaggression, because I just can't do it anymore. I was dealing with the burnout for a long period.

As Eng and Han (2018) explain, racial melancholia refers to 'sustained losses attendant to processes of immigration, assimilation, and racialisation for Asian immigrants and their second-generation children as well as depression and self-annihilation that emerge from this psychic state' (2018: 25). In the same vein, Hong (2020) uses 'minor feelings' to explain 'the racialised range of emotions that are negative, dysphoric, and therefore untelegenic, built from the sediments of everyday racial experience and the irritant of having one's perception of reality constantly questioned or dismissed' (2020: 55). Evidence of racial melancholia and minor feelings embodied by the women are sadly overwhelming in their narratives. A respondent in her late forties, though holding a senior management position, regretted over the loss she has sustained over the course of migration and decade-long career in the white institution:

> It makes me think about memories of my younger days when I was happier. It makes me question why I am here. I thought I would come here, receive education and be respected here for my work. But it is not the case.

This sense of pronounced hopelessness and disbelief in 'things will get better' and 'we have already come a long way' consumed me too when I reached the edge after enduring a year-long aggressive institutional racism campaign. Reading Eng & Han (2018) and Hong (2020) alongside listening to forty other Asian migrant women's stories provides a strong sense of validation knowing that my poor mental health condition and suicide attempt were not displays of self-indulgence and selfishness as some would judge. In fact, as Eng & Han (2018) explain, 'mourning without end' (2018: 25) is a common condition amongst racialized subjects. Present in the women's stories is their 'mourning without end' over impenetrable systems of colonialism, white supremacy and neoliberalism, white powers' insatiable appetite for dominance and capital-hoarding and their own sense of hopelessness in obtaining racial justice. A respondent in her mid-thirties from a refugee background, who has just completed a fixed-term professional job contract, revealed her acute sense of despair and 'mourning without end' when she wondered about her future:

> It's very painful. It's very hard to feel like you're not enough. My self-esteem is very low. I'm very anxious. I am very worried about the future

if I ever get a good opportunity. Very unhappy … I'm not optimistic … If I apply for a job again, are they gonna disqualify me because I'm not white Aussie? I have no energy to be honest, to put in an application and then get disqualified over my ethnicity, or my background, or my accent. This is what I'm afraid of happening in the future. It made me distrust. If I give 110% in any other role, are they gonna treat me with fairness, or they gonna hire some white Aussie person? If someone just because they are white or from specific background, they're gonna get preferred over me? It is making me feel like there is no point of pushing and going forward, or being optimistic about the future.

Since Asian immigrant women employees at the university are commonly perceived as well-adjusted, ambitious, successful and composed professionals, their racialization and racial injuries are not always apparent in popular imagination of racism and minoritization. The women in this study reported extensive costs of racism to their safety, livelihood, work life, career progression, financial status, access to permanent housing and home ownership, social relationships, physical and mental health and wellbeing and aspirations. What racial capitalism and racism fundamentally do to racialized subjects is to extract – extract land, minerals, resources, labour, knowledges, cultures, community ties, relationships, emotions and lives – whether it is in the forms of colonial empire expansion, industrialization or neoliberalism. There are several accounts concerning how respondents have worked for particular projects with senior white colleagues but were not given due credits in terms of publications' authorship, paid adequately or at all for labour and time they have put in, or provided with proper training, mentorship, support and learning opportunities. A respondent in her early thirties decided to return to her home country after living in Australia and being immersed in Australian higher education sector for more than a decade. She contrasted her work experience with women of colour supervisors versus white supervisors:

When I work with academics from Asian background, there is no power trip … We could have actual conversations even though we are not from the same cultural background. At least, when we talk about things, there is no colonial mindset or mentality. When I worked with Australian academics who are white, it's very much different. It was very top down. Also, I think, because of my work ethics from an Asian background, they have this expectation that they can give me things at the last minute because they know I will get things done to the best of my abilities and they do say that they respect or acknowledge my capabilities. But all they do is just push me to my limits, give me work and say I don't have time to do this, you do for me … and there is no acknowledgement of my work on publications and projects.

Being perceived as collected, hardworking, responsible and compliant Asian migrant women workers often means more work with poorer work conditions and no or limited avenues of redress. The bullying could also come in the forms of disregard for their welfare, well-being and career development. One respondent in her mid-thirties moved to Australia with her spouse and child to pursue her doctoral studies. She shared how she has been treated shabbily like a nobody by her white doctoral supervisors:

> Both of my supervisors were white Australians. They were not very supportive. It was a very bad experience. First of all, I think it started from cultural gaps because they have zero knowledge about my culture. They had no understanding, no interest to know about the context where I came from, my experiences and family background, nothing. They know nothing about me.

She complained about the control her supervisors had over her from limiting work opportunities, dictating work schedules, curtailing travel plans for home visits and withholding rudimentary level of career progression support. Several respondents also reported other forms of relational bullying where their compliance with the imposed myth of a hardworking, responsible and dependable Asian migrant woman worker brought them undesirable anxieties and insecurities from white peers:

> When nobody wanted to put their hand up for certain work, I put
> my hand up to do it. People would think she is an Asian and so
> that's expected of her to do that. Australian white colleagues think
> Asians like me want to outperform and be striving. But that is not
> the case. It is just that no one wants to do that work so I get the
> work done. White colleagues think you were trying to outperform
> them and snatch their rice bowl if you work harder or stay back to
> work more.

Passive aggressive racialized treatments by white peers followed suit
for this first-generation migrant respondent in her forties who held a
senior professional position:

> I was usually at my desk during lunch. A white woman colleague
> walked in and asked me, 'Has your supervisor unleashed you?' I did
> not understand what she meant at first. I said, 'I don't understand'.
> Then she explained, 'You know like a little dog, only your supervisor
> could unleash you right since you are still at your desk.' When I heard
> it, I felt horrible, very uncomfortable and very very sad.

It is undoubtedly hard to call out such casual racism at a relational
and social level. Nevertheless, the women have come to bear racial
injuries and trauma in their everyday work reality. What it also means
is that they are constantly required to be hypervigilant in their career
moves: Do I work hard to fulfil the expectations of myths imposed on
my racialized, ornamentalized body? Do I tone my achievements and
ambitions down so that white colleagues will not feel threatened and,
in turn, lash out their anxieties on me? How much whiteness should
I do to be deemed as good enough for a job or promotion but not so
much whiteness that they think I am inauthentic, pedestrian and not
exotic and intriguing enough? One respondent in her late thirties who
has been living and working in Australia for eight years bemoaned over
her undulating career pathway as a non-white woman academic and
pointed out the social capital accumulation and career development
opportunities her white colleagues enjoyed:

It took me five years since graduation to get my first job. All my white friends who did PhD together with me got jobs immediately. They had a very different mentorship. They had a very different support system. They came from a very different world. You know they had access to the systemic language that I had no access to … My career has been definitely affected by all of that.

The extraction and debilitation the women encountered wore them down. Beneath a collected, successful and well-adjusted front, almost every respondent I spoke with revealed that they suffered from significant health issues. Some of their health problems include cancer, complex post-traumatic stress disorder, depression, anxiety, panic attacks, burn-out, fibromyalgia, hyperacidity, chronic pains, endometriosis, hypothyroidism and irritable bowel syndrome. They attributed their health troubles to racism-related trauma, distress and stress at the workplace.

Myth of 'being homogenous and safe'

I showed in class this cleverly done video clip on a satire making fun of my brown accent while critiquing whiteness and racism in Australia … and I could see this young brown man look at me with such hatred. I noticed it the first class he didn't engage with me when I was talking to him … Then a complaint came in saying I am racist to white people … the way the complaint was written and I thought, okay, so this is misogyny. And it's also a person of colour who's unable to see the power over them because they are completely whitewashed by this white norm. And I was challenging that norm by making fun of myself, and that was just too hard because if someone's insecure about themselves as a young brown man surrounded by whiteness and conscious about the accent and this show is making fun of that accent … it just shows how the system works to actually perpetuate this kind of whiteness as the norm … where we suffer racism from non-white people, and sometimes people from your own.

Oftentimes, there is an assumption and expectation that minority peoples and communities bound by marginalizations, albeit difference in intersectional forms and manifestations, would be in solidarity and have one another's back. Some of the respondents in this study explained that was not always the case. The respondent above and several others related the double layer of violence and profound sense of betrayal when they encountered lateral violence from fellow people of colour co-workers and students who wield the oppressor's weapons against them. They shared that the shock to their bodily systems was oftentimes more pronounced when they experienced racialized violence from people of colour than when they encountered racism by white powers. It is perhaps a harder pill to swallow when minoritized people apply the master's tools on other minoritized people since we expect a certain level of understanding, empathy and solidarity considering they have also been subjected to marginalization. However, what the narratives present is the heterogeneity of minoritized subjects. The study's empirical data debunk the myth of minoritized subjects as homogenous in their marginalized positions and responses to oppressions. The findings also show how minoritized subjects do not always offer a safety net against whiteness and racialized oppressions.

At the point of writing this book, I was reading about Miss Major, a Black trans-revolutionary, and her activism work and contemplated upon the lateral violence my respondents and I were body slammed with. Miss Major advises 'how getting liberated requires being aware of how oppression can cause trans people to adopt the ways of their oppressors – that the sometimes vicious competition and gaslighting in the trans community comes from the trauma, poverty and class oppression that many trans people face' (Meronek & Major 2023: 29). What is illuminating in her insights based on decades of advocating for trans-African American people is how minoritized people in their bid for survival may compel them to not only play by the rules of the oppressor's game but also act an accomplice to exact violence the same way on other minoritized people. The latter may not have done so deliberately and consciously but rather acting out as a response and reaction to the oppression they have been subjected to. Ultimately, the lateral violence they commit to other oppressed people is a result of the struggles and debilitation they face but unfortunately reinforce the dominance of the oppressor since the oppressor's logic is reproduced through the lateral violence the oppressed commit against each other.

A particular respondent in her mid-forties, who had moved with her family to Australia when she was a young child, lamented over her work experience with fellow people of colour colleagues:

> My experiences with racism have come from people of colour who think that they are committed to decolonization, diversity and everything … They are like I'm a man of color myself. I've experienced so much race, so blah blah blah, so they will use their own position to deflect … the identity politics would be used … I guess men who were making a lot of mileage out of their post-colonial credentials, but they can't bear it when women criticize them. They insist on a kind of a racialised gender that is also terrible. There's so much racism and sexism … a really strong misogyny.

The respondent described how some people of colour co-workers engaged in identity politics and leveraged upon their minority identities to gain capital and privileges by enrolling into the white academy's decolonizing, postcolonial, multiculturalism and cultural diversity projects. Instead of toppling unjust structures of colonial legacy, their collusion with the institution's white race-making and whitewashing efforts supported the status quo of unequal power relations and in return earned them power dividends. Like their white master, they did not hold back in mobilizing their power to stamp out opposition so as to hold on to the capital they have amassed. This brings us back to Miss Major's observation on racialized people of colour learning the ways of the oppressor and out of their own racialized trauma, survival instincts, self-protection tactics and competition for rations, welding the oppressor's weapons to exact violence against other minoritized people. In this respondent's case, her men of colour colleagues regarded her with a complexly interwoven lens of racialization and sexualization and exerted patriarchal control over her at the workplace. Her situation is certainly not unique.

Other respondents related how some men of colour colleagues would treat them as maids and personal assistants and expected them to carry out secretarial and housework that were often not within their job scope. Interestingly, the women's narratives also brought out a usual relationship dynamic where men of colour co-workers in their reluctance to approach white colleagues directly with their questions and requests would sometimes turn to the Asian migrant women respondents to act as an intermediary brokering the unequal racial power relations. This extra, invisible interrelation and emotional labour the women have come to bear because of their racialized and gendered positions goes unnoticed far too often. A senior academic respondent in her mid-forties complained about this unpleasant encounter with a man of colour co-worker:

> After the meeting, he contacted me on social messaging and asked me to check if one of my colleagues has replied to their email. I asked him to contact my colleague directly and I knew that my colleague was very responsive. But he still asked me to remind my colleague to reply to their email. I was the only female academic on my side. There must be something here right? He knew I am also an academic. Coming from a patriarchal culture, being a younger looking woman, you get a lot of silly questions and requests. I was so angry that I wrote to him and told him to contact my colleague directly. I told him that I was not my colleague's personal assistant. I feel that this is racism and sexism. If I were a white woman, he would not ask me to do that. Even now talking about it, I am very pissed off.

Such sentiments, 'If I were a white man, they would not say this to me' and 'If I were a white woman, they would not ask me to do this', were commonly heard in this study. The women made these comments not just in response to racialized treatments from white people but also lateral violence they encountered from people of colour colleagues at the workplace.

A few other respondents related that they sadly suffered lateral racialized violence from women of colour colleagues who engaged in gaslighting to gate keep borders of whiteness by asking the usual dismissive questions: *Are you being too sensitive? Are you overthinking? Are you overreacting? How about calm down, just let it go and practise self-care?* In the process, the latter like the men of colour accomplices mentioned above safe keep the privileges they have earned through working hard to assimilate, toe the line and ascend the career ladder. A respondent in her late sixties, who has worked in the academy for four decades, made an astute observation about how women of colour co-workers have learned the ways of the oppressor and dutifully and compliantly followed the oppressor's rules to become the oppressor's accomplice strengthening existing power structures and subjugating oppressed subjects in the lower rung of the racial hierarchy:

> Women of colour in power … they think in order to succeed, this is what I need to do. Such racism is unreflected upon in the academy because people think if they were educators and academics, they won't be racist. People of colour who suffer racism, they either become energetic in fighting racism or they become the oppressor themselves to survive the system.

Such lateral violence has also regrettably been present in the classroom, where a few respondents related how they experienced racialized and gendered bullying from students of colour. The stark contrast between how the same group of minoritized students behaved towards them and in the presence of white man teaching staff, sometimes more junior-ranking and less qualified than the Asian migrant women academics concerned, did not pass them. One first-generation migrant respondent in her mid-forties related how she would frequently face racialized and sexualized treatment by students of colour from her cultural and linguistic background. 'What idiotic remarks and brain-damaging commentary did that woman just make? Talking to herself!', a student wrote on the open chat during an online class. Instead of writing it in English for the entire cohort to read, the student of colour wrote it in his home language that was known to the respondent. The latter reflected that the deliberate choice of language by the student concerned was to get her attention, restrict the audience of that insult to their common cultural community and thereby seek to affect the respondent's reputation in their common cultural community. What the student achieved through expressing the verbally abusive remark in his home language was marking out his comfort zone by the use of his home language and bringing those present who shared his home language into a social space where he could mobilize with ease gender power differentials familiar to him. In that social space where his racialized position was suspended and social status momentarily restored by his cultural and gender positions, he felt emboldened to exact sexism and misogyny at a fellow woman of his cultural and language background albeit her professional position as his teacher. In that space, he was not the racialized other but a dominant man with patriarchal dividends. The respondent complained:

> If I were a white male professor, this student would not have written in English that this man is talking nonsense ... it would not have triggered the same emotional reaction in this student. If the student were to say something in English, he would be exposed to a larger audience. The student would not have said it in English ... The comment was so bad because I was only referred and reduced to a woman, and the student chose to write in my language because he know I understand it.

Another first-generation migrant respondent in her thirties holding an early career academic staff position also related similar encounters with disruptive behaviour by students of colour:

> A few male students of colour were very disruptive and I told them to leave. They wouldn't leave and I had to get the security to come and get them to leave. I think they are not used to having a brown woman telling them what to do. I don't think they would do that to a white person.

There have been scholarly and popular discourses on internalized racism, racial self-hatred and internalized oppression to make sense of the ill treatment, hostility and bullying racialized minorties subject other racially marginalized people to (Pheterson 1986; David 2014; Hong 2020; Whyman et al. 2021). These discussions tend to focus on the individual subject that has been contaminated by the oppressor's values and beliefs about themselves and the oppressed subjects. No doubt that it is possible that the oppressed subjects, as Miss Major has observed, have learned the ways of the oppressor and enacted violence against other marginalized people. However, rather than focusing on marginalized subjects' internalized racism and remedial actions to correct internalized racism and self-fulfilling prophetical behaviours, I am more interested in moving away from an individualistic approach to discuss how certain structural conditions promote violence laterally and horizontally among oppressed minoritized populations.

Taking a historicized perspective helps us understand the persistent colonial and racial capitalist practices and orders in present moments in the academy. The colonial legacy and racial hierarchy we have come to inherit continue to shape global orders and every aspect of the society we are located in. The settler-colonial system introduced a racial hierarchy that not only placed European Anglo-Saxon populations at the top rung but also stratified minoritized populations according to colonialists' arbitrary definition and ranking of humanity. The racial hierarchal system therefore already set colonizied Indigenous peoples and minoritized non-white subjects to compete against each another and among themselves for resources the oppressor majority permitted them to have and demanded that they must exact lateral violence in order to survive and secure whatever resources they could have.

Minoritized Asian immigrant populations embedded in Australian settler-colonial society though deployed collectively to be settlers are far from being homogenous and regional racial histories, hierarchies and geopolitics shape their relation dynamics. Tze Ming Mok's (2022) discussion on black and white Asians is useful here in illustrating pronounced racial hierarchies within Asian immigrant settlers in white settler-colonial societies. Mok's (2022) research does not seek to reinforce biological, essentialist race concept and create racial categories based on phenotypical traits. Rather, their discussion centres Asian migrant-settlers' proximity and relation to white settler state's racial capitalist projects. When Asians are Black, they are further removed from capital and more politically aligned with Black African diasporic anti-racism activism (Mok 2022). As Cheng (2019) also points out, Black and brown categories are used as 'denominating categories of injury' (2019: xi) in relation to their colonized, racialized and subjugated conditions. When Asians are white, they display model minority attributes and enjoy honorary whiteness through active participation in buttressing white supremacy (Mok 2022). In Mok's research, their respondents have referred disenfranchised brown, South Asians as Black Asians, while East Asians with internalized model minority myth and honorary white privilege are referred to as white Asians (Mok 2022). It is however not to say that South Asians will be not white or East Asians cannot be Black. Mok's analysis calls out the elephant in the room which is the unequal racialized power relations within heterogenous Asian migrant-settler populations in white settler-states and the complicity of white Asians in elevating whiteness and debilitating blackness.

Damagingly, marginalized subjects have long been recruited, whitewashed and co-opted to be an accessory for extractive colonial and racial capitalized subjects. For example, during British colonial rule in Australia, Aboriginal leaders were recruited by British colonial governors and landowners as 'black trackers' and 'Native Police' to control Aboriginal peoples and consequently 'created tension and newly-formed hierarchies within communities, undermining Aboriginal social structures' (Whyman et al. 2021: 185). This co-optation tactic remains intact where minoritized subjects such as Aboriginal peoples and immigrant-settlers continue to be recruited into settler-colonial structures and nation-state systems and deployed as cogs in the machinery to subordinate the broader minority populations while safeguarding the white majority's power, privileges and interests. The tentacles of racial capitalist and neoliberal systems have extended so far and deep that there is not much space to wiggle, avoid complicity and resist. It is therefore not surprising when this respondent in her early thirties who has settled well with securing Australian citizenship, home ownership and a permanent, well-paid employment would support a settler-colonial system that even though has racialized and minoritized her, rewarded her with material comforts and capital for her diligence, obedience and compliance. The first-generation immigrant respondent even went as far as reproaching other minority immigrant-settlers for not putting in more effort to assimilate:

> A lot of friends around me, they are quite reluctant to fit in and understand Australia and local culture, and how things work here. They are very stuck in their own little culture group and not willing to step out of their comfort zone to really explore or communicate with the local white people. And I think there can be an aspect of that lack of contributions from Asians.

She opined that Asian immigrants should make greater effort in walking out of their comfort zones away from their own cultural groups, learning local cultures and integrating themselves into mainstream society. The lateral violence she unknowingly implicated herself in reveals a particular context her immigrant cohort is situated in. Eng & Han (2018) discuss in their work the case studies of Generation Y, millennial (1981–96) parachute children where the latter migrate for educational pursuits in hope of permanent residency and work opportunities. The authors use the case studies of parachute children to illustrate the manifestation of what they call racial dissociation and 'racial nowhere' where their case studies are disconnected from broader racial histories. In the case of this respondent, she appears to display racial dissociation through her indifference towards racial histories, denial of whiteness and racism, disdain towards members of her own racial and cultural group, critiques of and dissociation from them and diligence in instating her social status as an equal, participating and productive member of the Australian society. The self-annihilation (Eng & Han 2018) comes in the form of disciplining, controlling and pushing self to get rid of former cultures and practices and acquire, imitate and resemble local ways such that their racial, pathologized self does not figure or is carefully concealed. This survival tactic may not be carried out consciously though. By discussing self-assimilation, self-loathing and internalized racism the respondent has displayed, the aim is not to cast an individualistic lens and activate popular positive psychology remedies for fixing individual behaviours and promoting self-love, empowerment and agency. Instead, I seek to provide an explanation on the historicized and contemporary racialized contexts that shape different cohorts of minoritized migrant-settlers' responses to racialized environments, often compelling them to disassociate, assimilate and display white majority's ways for survival, safety, stability and capacitation. Another early academic career respondent in her early forties shared how her man of colour colleague advised her to make self-modification by changing her name and going along with the white ways so as to make life easier for herself. This colleague also unfortunately made racial assumptions of her cultural backgrounds the way her white colleagues have done:

> He suggested to me, in a sort of half-joking way, that I anglicise my name. I just remember thinking it's not a joke. I really didn't expect it to come from someone who is also Asian and has experienced the difficulties of being Asian in the workspace. A lot of white people often mistake my name, so he was suggesting that it might just make things easier if I went ahead with it. He also once made a comment about my community. We were organizing a conference, and deciding on the venue people. He made this off-hand comment about my community drinks a lot of alcohol and promptly turned to me and expect me to reconfirm.

As Miss Major has observed, oppression can cause oppressed people to adopt the ways of their oppressors (Meronek & Major 2023).

4

Happy diversity: Myths and realities of corporate diversity and inclusion

Happy diversity

– By Beth Yahp for Ee Ling Quah
(unpublished, reproduced here with
Beth Yahp's permission)

Two
white
ram-men,
towering.
Diversity steps,
candy-coloured concrete rainbow.

Smile!
One
step at
a time! One
Asian woman shows
we're candy-coloured rainbows too.

We're
chef
kissing
her home-made
curry. Her world-honed
fury, not so much. She dragon

speaks
her
name. She
words hot! Too
hot for the ram-men
media smiling diversity.
Ram
say,
ram do.
Once rainbowed,
who needs to know her
name? Her body's bullseye enough

for
the
photo
op. Hey! We're
good! We listen! We
inaugurate happy happy

di
ver
sity!
Your vibrant
multi-colours are
so pretty. And, mwah, your curry!

Don't
say
racist
– that's racist!
The ram-men ram home
truths home. Diversity, baby,

we're
all
rainbows
now. Your barbed
incivility
crosses the line. Hey! We're fragile

too!
White
ram-men
scissor the
red ribbon she holds.
Wide smiling happy happy while

her
words
red hot,
her fire
dragon's body, so
rainbow pretty, bullseyes them back

Beth Yaph, an acclaimed fiction and non-fiction author of noteworthy works such as *The red pearl and other stories* (2017) and *Eat first, talk later* (Yaph 2015), poet and academic, penned and gifted me this powerful poem after listening to my bizarre stories on institutional and everyday racisms. Yaph's poem reveals how white people like our cultural cuisine, our alignment with their version of modernity and most importantly our smiles and submissiveness. But if we even dare to be 'uncivil' and 'bulleyes them back', there will be undesirable and punitive consequences for us. The poem encapsulates all too pertinently and profoundly the amalgamated racialization and sexualization Asian migrant women and more widely, Indigenous women and women of colour experience at the workplace.

Myth of essentialized and compartmentalized selves in identity-focused EDI

> Employers have diversity obligations. They do not understand who we are, so they're basically asking us to racialise ourselves. In my experience, now that there is a lot of pressure on workplaces to diversify and address race issues and decolonization and stuff like that, they will jump at anything … Look here we are, we're doing it, we're doing that. You look, we go to these brown women. We're going to treat them like shit, and we're going to expect them to racialize themselves so that we can be comfortable with them, but the minute they get too assertive, we're going to get really upset. But nevertheless, look at our photographs. You know we've got brown women. But the minute you upset their own sense of hierarchy … they just melt down … I wasn't behaving Asian enough for them … They desire all of us to behave in really essentialist ways. And when I wasn't doing that I got in such trouble.

This respondent's complaint hit the nail about Equity, Diversity and Inclusion (EDI) initiatives at the workplace. The main problem of corporatized, compartmentalized identity-focused EDI lies with essentializing, disintegrating and compartmentalizing one's multiple selves and often expecting one to perform and conform to constructed myths of each identity category mainly for corporate branding exercises and human resource management purposes. As what the respondent indicated, when minoritized subjects are recruited into diversity and inclusion campaigns, their employer is asking them to self-racialize so that they are distinctly culturally and linguistically diverse from the white majority. When they comply, they make good poster children for publicity efforts to boast the university's success in being inclusive, diverse and not racist. They get a nod from their employer and subsequently stand a chance of being rewarded in their career.

However, the respondent warned that they must not to be too different that would ignite a certain level of self-consciousness, which might in turn instigate a revolt against dominant powers. The respondent went on to describe this diversity and inclusion game as the 'new prison of "okay, we'll accept you but perform your difference, perform your gratefulness, perform your desire to make us happy, be our audience, laugh at our jokes, never tell us we're making a big mistake, because that's another thing". The respondent was spot on in exposing the reductive approach dominant powers employ to confine minoritized subjects in aesthetic display of exoticism for generation of profits, set clearly demarcated borders of diversity and inclusion parade and send warnings of punitive measures should subjugated subjects dare to complain and stray. As the respondent pointed out, the institution or any dominant power has no interest in knowing and understanding their minoritized subjects. Another respondent I spoke with echoed the violating effects of such superficial presentation of cultural diversity where there is no genuine interest in understanding differences:

> There is a flattening or an essentialism that the person of colour in the room, can speak of all of their society ... they want you to speak for all of the Asians. What do I say? When they see, 'Oh, here's an Asian. What do you think and like?' I become the diversity spokesperson.

What such a narrow and reductive approach behind many seemingly well-intentioned EDI initiatives does is to essentialize other and subjugate minoritized subjects with the ultimate outcome of protecting the dominance of the majority. One respondent complained:

> I really think we need to rethink what we call cultural diversity, cultural understanding or cultural competence, because the moment they see us as an object to understand, we are already seen as different and other ... I don't think they know how to really engage with diversity.

In the identity-focused EDI space, humanity is narrowly defined by and forcefully confined to static, bounded identity categories. The latter are imagined to be monolithic, neatly compartmentalized and self-contained. Each identity category group focusing on specific areas of marginalization along the lines of gender, sexuality and culturally diversity is presumed to have obtained 'homogeneity or consensus where there is none, and in doing so enact relations of domination, policing as well as forgetting differences' (Kwon & Nguyen 2016). The ways in which colonial and essentialist understandings of gender, sexuality and cultural heritage manifest in the various well-meaning community groups are arguably problematic, counter-productive and even violent. I would argue that these EDI initiatives sometimes do more harm in reinforcing myths and unequal power structures than good in improving lives. For example, when corporations – including universities – advocate for gender equality, their approach often narrowly focuses on improving women's productivity and representation in leadership positions. It's not that these concerns are unimportant, but they cannot be the only things that occupy the EDI space. It is often an unthinking reaction to reduce gender equity priorities to considering and solving women's issues and saving them as if gender were a synonym for women or, more specifically, white, straight, cisgender women. Only a select group of women's interests and concerns are prioritised and positioned as the point of reference and benchmark for members of other gender minority groups to identify with and struggle alongside. At best, corporatized gender equality policies and efforts advocate for these women's concerns and needs. At worst, they send a message that other human bodies – such as (but not limited to) Indigenous women, women of colour, queer women, trans, non-binary, genderqueer and agender individuals, queer men, men of colour, Indigenous men and bodies labelled as disabled – do not matter. To be clear, I am not platforming identity politics here to make a case for other identity groups to be recognized in the competition for access. On the contrary, I am interested in unpacking the multiple layers of violence in corporate EDI space driven by identity categorization, recognition of certain selected priority groups and controlling and policing of differences based on the dominator's terms.

Corporate gender equity initiatives' persistent and reductive treatment of gender in binary terms reinforces the maintenance of two neat, clean categories of humanity – men and women. The resulting advocacy stemmed from white benevolence and inclusion/exclusion logic is then skewed towards helping or saving members of the 'weaker' group, namely women in a patriarchal society. The latter is allowed to be let in and access resources on the condition that they play by the rules of the game and will be rewarded if they play the game well. Ultimately, the goal of gender equity efforts appears to be about enhancing white, cisgender, heterosexual women's productivity at work and training them in white masculine leadership so that they can perform like their white, cisgender, heterosexual men counterparts to boost the company's business. Many seemingly progressive corporations, including universities, have a weak grasp of multiple genders and the coloniality of the gender binary and heteropatriarchal systems. Whenever I remind colleagues, including senior management, in my different capacities as a gender and sexuality scholar, as an anti-colonial feminist activist and, formerly, as the Chair of LGBTIQA+ Ally Network, that we need to take on an anti-colonial approach to the work of gender and sexuality equity in the university and employ a multiple genders and sexualities system, I often get a puzzled look. It's as if they cannot fathom how gender can mean more than just cisgender men and women and how sexuality is dynamic and not confined to heterosexuality and homosexuality. In my years of classroom and research activism, I find myself work harder to advocate for an understanding of multiple genders, sexualities and sex characteristics and remind students and colleagues how the colonial legacy of cisgender binaries and heteronormativity hurt us all, including white heterosexual men, albeit unevenly by entrapping us in the strict confines of identity, role and performance and punishing those who dare to wander off.

Another problematic and violent aspect of such reductive, essentialist and identity-focused approach in the EDI space is the neat compartmentalization of identity-based diversity work. The common focus areas of corporate EDI efforts include gender equity, where the emphasis is mainly about white cisgender heterosexual women; LGBTIQA+ rainbow alliance and allyship, whose advocacy is driven by white queer people's concerns and understandings of queerness; cultural competence, diversity and well-being focuses mainly on Indigenous peoples and multicultural communities who are not white. Each of these diversity spaces is designed for singular identity markers and confined to particular identity groups. It feels as if we are being asked to peel off a layer of our integrated selves to enter each space and present only that specific, static identity marker to participate in its activities. What does it mean for someone like me, a queer migrant woman in a white settler-colonial society? It means I have to enter the gender equity space to talk about women's empowerment and leadership, move to the LGBTIQA+ space to shout rainbow pride at Mardi Gras parade and finally to the cultural competence space to teach white people about race and how not to be unconsciously bias. I find myself very busy doing multiple diversity works in these neatly defined spaces. In each of these spaces, parts of me do not get validated and, in fact, feel patronized and violated when I am in any particular EDI space. For example, when I am in the rainbow pride space, no one seems to care about the racism and xenophobia I encounter alongside with queerphobia. Similarly, when I am in the gender equity space, the white women champions carefully avoid any mention of colonialism, race and heteronormativity. Are our lives so easily dissected and contained? When I walk along the street and encounter harassment, is it sexism, racism, xenophobia or queerphobia? Or could it be all of these? The fact that I do not know how I should frame my complaint and to whom I could file my complaint reveals the limitations of existing identity-focused systems.

Queer theory scholars like Paul Preciado (2013, 2020) and Jasbir Puar (2017) have also argued against identity politics where concerns with identification including identity formation, classification, reproduction, oppression, struggle, recognition and politics – whether intentionally as part of our activist politics or unconsciously as a result of broader socialization and normalization – is based on the assumption that identities are essentialist, static and bounded. As minoritized subjects struggle to get their identities represented and included, they oftentimes end up in divisive situations as the premise of identity and representation politics is always based on competition for the dominant majority's recognition and limited resources the majority is willing to dispense.

In addition, existing EDI programmes being compartmentalized in reductive identity-based areas namely, gender, LGBTIQA+ and cultural diversity create a politics and practice of difference that, while recognizes multiple standpoints, perspectives, subject positions, identities and contexts, evades the coloniality, racial capitalism and whiteness that produces the oppressive material conditions that afflict them collectively albeit unevenly and unequally (Moreton-Robinson 2020a). Historical contexts shaping contemporary unequal conditions and ecologies that continue to control and discipline human bodies and lives based on the same colonial and racial capitalist logics get ignored. What identity-driven EDI programmes do then is to dehistorize, decontexualize, highlight, judge and manage differences according to the institution's definitions of gender, sexuality and cultural identities and thresholds for differences. In these EDI programs, 'whiteness remains the invisible omnipresent norm' (Moreton-Robinson 2020a: xix). In respective EDI spaces, mainly gender, sexuality and cultural diversity, whiteness as dominance and privilege are not discussed as contributing factors to their gender, sexuality and racial oppressions. Instead, gender, sexuality and cultural identities are made visible and differentiated to highlight identity-based oppressions, and the resulting advocacy efforts are directed at promoting and celebrating their different identities. For example, in the Australian university context, gender equity space is largely dominated by white women who 'are not represented to themselves as being white; instead they position themselves as variously classed, sexualised, aged and abled' (Moreton-Robinson 2020a: xxv). In the LGBTIQA+ space, whiteness and racial capitalism are also invisible and unproblematic to white queer people who are beneficiaries of white racial privilege. Instead, heteronormativity is framed as the sole enemy as if the naturalization and normativity of heterosexuality is unrelated to its colonial roots. In the cultural and linguistically diversity space, racial hierarchy between the white majority and othered non-white populations and within the multicultural, diasporic communities is often flattened. Instead of centring activism against racial inequalities and injustice, this deracialized space foregrounds cultural traditions and festivals to celebrate harmony and unity in diversity and as a result orientalizes, exoticizes and ornamentalizes themselves and reinforces invisibility of white racial privilege. Nira Yuval-Davis (2012) warns that the 'emphasis on the importance of the lives of the most marginal elements in society can sometimes collude with the attempts of hegemonic centers to remain opaque while at the same time maintaining the surveillance of marginal elements in society' (2012:48). In each of these EDI spaces where specific identity differences and struggles are emphasized and foregrounded, there is a lack of attention on their relationality with colonial, racial capitalist and white supremacist historical and contemporary projects. There is also a glaring absence of interrogation of their implications in these projects. These self-contained spaces complicity serve to authorize and police borders of gender, sexuality and multiculturalism as determined by invisible, natural and unmarked white powers. With racial inequalities whitewashed in this culturally and linguistically diverse and artificially harmonious space, normative structures of white powers remain invisible, undisrupted and omnipresent. Lisa Lowe (2015) reminds that the focus should be about examining the 'differentially situated histories of indigeneity, slavery, industry, trade and immigration [that] give rise to linked, but not identical, genealogies of liberalism', 'relation across differences rather than equivalence' and 'the convergence of asymmetries rather than the imperatives of identity' (2015: 11).

I turn to Paul Preciado's (2020) position on disidentification and anti-identity politics to consider how we may transform and reorganize the corporate EDI space into a collective solidarity platform for social justice and sustainability. Preciado (2020) explains clearly the model of identity politics is in fact the modern model of colonial taxonomy, heteronormative taxonomy and sexual difference and argues why we need to abandon identification and identity politics:

> What does it mean to live in a particular place? Under what conditions is someone allowed to live in a particular place? This of course comes from discussions around migration, but also the changing conditions

of the contemporary city and how capitalism is constantly segmenting spaces and making them impossible to inhabit. This might be a physical place – a city or a territory or a nation – or the place of the family, domesticity, maternity, gender, love. All those positions are also defined under very strict conditions…

What I'm trying to do is to think the transformation of contemporary democracy without, or beyond, the model of identity politics. And I think this is crucial, because the model of identity politics is also the modern model of colonial taxonomy, of heteronormative taxonomy, of sexual difference.

For Preciado (2020), disidentification is key here in addressing contemporary ecological crises we are facing:

I no longer identify as gay or lesbian, as heterosexual or homosexual, as male or female. I'm somewhere else and I am not the only one. I think that now, because of both the ecological crisis and an array of new technologies that have completely changed the way that subjectivity and collective social living are constructed, we cannot continue to organise in terms of identity politics.

Instead of investing in identity struggle and recognition, Preciado (2020) urges us to think about our existence in terms of political relationality and activism to be based on transversal alliance of all living things:

We are in a moment of planetary transition. We are moving into a different epistemology that might – at least this is what I try to fight for – give political recognition to any living body without demanding identification in terms of gender, sexuality or even differences like human or animal. We will soon be confronted with the fact that we have to recognise our rivers and oceans as political beings, as many Indigenous communities have long done. This will completely shake the traditional taxonomies around which we have organised politics.

Taking on an intersectional approach means we need to acknowledge and oppose coloniality, racial capitalism, neoliberalism, patriarchy and heteronormativity – systems that simultaneously and complexly compel bodies to capacitate according to dominant logics for survival and debilitate bodies, organisms and environments that fail to do so. It is impossible to write, speak and teach about race, gender, sexuality, inequality and injustice without making loud noises about broader structures that debilitate and oppress human lives at constrictive intersections of colonialism, racial capitalism, neoliberalism, heteronormativity and patriarchy.

Myth of intersectionality

In response to critiques of diversity and inclusion programs as being singularly focused on particular individual social identities in separate, compartmentalized focus areas, the buzzword of 'intersectionality' would be thrown in the mix to appease critics and minorities who feel that their needs and concerns have not been meaningfully recognized and addressed. I am all for intersectional approaches, but not when intersectionality gets co-opted as yet another corporate branding effort to boast inclusion and diversity without meaningful and truthful interrogation of histories, structural conditions and systems of inequalities. Sirma Bilge (2013) highlights that 'intersectionality, originally focused on transformative and counter-hegemonic knowledge production and radical politics of social justice, has been *commodified and colonized* for neoliberal regimes' (2013:407). Far too often, well-meaning identity-focused activists, diversity workers and grassroots organizations think that by using the 'intersectionality' buzzword, and recruiting, including and representing more gender, sexuality and culturally diverse people as poster children, they have done 'intersectionality'. It is as if by throwing into the mix a few women, people of colour, LGBTIQA+ people and people with disabilities, it will be enough to demonstrate how all-inclusive and 'intersectional' we are. Better still, if we get hold of someone like me, who embodies additive marginalized identities – queer, Asian, woman – we hit the jackpot for 'intersectionality'. EDI programmes set up to be 'intersectional' only end up compelling target beneficiaries to prove their multifold oppressions by listing their minority identities. At an EDI event, I witnessed a diversity worker claim they have at least seven intersecting identities and appear to demonstrate to the white people at the meeting how multiply marginalized they are. The non-white diversity worker's effort of 'Look at me! I am more oppressed and worthy of your attention' seems to suggest that minoritized subjects must wear multiple badges of marginalization to improve their qualifications as an 'intersectional' minority person deserving of recognition and support.

Critics of misunderstanding, appropriation and corporatization of intersectionality have long established that intersectionality is not simply adding up multiple fixed and essentialist identities to argue for the degree of marginalization and woundedness individual subjects may experience and their level of deservedness in accessing supportive resources (Puar 2012; Nash 2016; 2019a). The additive 'intersectional' approach is fundamentally still driven by a focus on identity and representation politics, which does not dismantle unequal power structures but in fact conceals subjects' political relationality and embeddedness in unequal power structures and upholds the interests of white supremacy, colonialism and racial capitalism (Christoffersen & Emejulu 2023). As Chandra Talpade Mohanty (2013) observes, power differences get domesticated through 'transforming systemic projects of resistance into commodified, private acts of rebellion' and this 'proliferation of depoliticised multiplicities' has become 'a hallmark of neoliberal intellectual landscapes' (2013: 968). The additive identitarian 'intersectional' EDI programmes often unfortunately degenerate into an Oppression Olympics as Ange-Marie Hancock (2011) puts it. The goal of the Oppression Olympics participants is to emerge victorious in this identity and representation political game by showing how much one is more oppressed and deserving of recognition and benevolence than another minoritized subject and community. What is constitutive of the Oppression Olympics is the hierarchy of oppressions and allocation of resources based on the hierarchy. The questions to ask here are: Who gets to rank? How is the hierarchy determined? Why do marginalized subjects have to compete for resources? Intersectionality in this case has been appropriated as a racial capitalist tool to manage minoritized subjects and resource allocation. Such a corporate 'intersectional' approach is still bound up with identity categorization and struggles and therefore fuels identity politics where essentialist ideas of minoritized subjects are upheld and encourage the latter to display multiple oppressed identities for competition of recognition and resources. Patricia Hill Collins (1990) warns against mechanisms to construct hierarchies of oppression and emphasizes that 'decentering the dominant group is essential' (1990: 237). What colonization and corporatization of intersectionality do, like other EDI efforts, is to elide white powers while attempting to give attention to marginalization and inequalities. Even if a non-hierarchal approach is taken, reducing inequities to merely differences and pretending the dominant centre is absent and not responsible for inequities and injustices is only going to reinforce the centre's opaqueness, invisibility, surveillance, control and power (Yuval-Davis 2012).

EDI programmes, while claiming to be 'intersectional' in their advocacy efforts, persist in being identitarian and make the typical mistake of operating based on inclusion/exclusion logic. What can be observed in the EDI space is that in the attempt to do intersectionality, diversity workers actively recruit minoritized subjects with multiple minority identity markers to demonstrate how inclusive their efforts and diverse their beneficiary constituents are. A respondent understood her purpose well:

> I think my employment is certainly seen as a very positive thing for the school, as a gay Asian woman, and for a while I was the poster child, you know. and I'm in talks about just being.

As Sara Ahmed observes, 'the language of intersectionality is now associated with diversity' (Ahmed 2012: 14). Maria Carbin and Sara Edenheim (2013) also lament that intersectionality 'has moved from being a sign of threat and conflict to (white) feminism to a consensus-creating signifier that not only made the concept successful but also enabled an institutionalisation of a liberal, "all-inclusive" feminism based on a denial of power as constitutive for all subjects' (2013: 234). Often, I find myself busy being the poster child sandwiched between powerful white men as I cut ribbons for the launch of rainbow steps while simultaneously being injured by merciless punitive measures for speaking out against white supremacy, colonialism and institutional racism. Another respondent of the study complained about how she has been often recruited to be the 'intersectional' diversity poster child for her university's gender equity campaigns but at same time is expected to only perform according to racialized expectations imposed on her and not beyond the confines of racialized borders defined for her in the EDI space or elsewhere in the institution:

> On International Women's Day, when they needed my face, my yellow face and my ethnicity, they put me on the screen. They put me on a show, and asked me to say some nice things about how great Australia is, so they use me for their own promotion, and when they don't need me, and they're setting me up and backstabbing me … if I'm strong, then you call me a bully. If I'm not strong, smiley, and then I'll become like, you know, a smiling Asian woman … this very superficial level of respecting diversity and inclusion … creates this ongoing sexism and racism.

What this respondent's narrative shows is that no matter how 'intersectional' and 'diverse' our EDI efforts appear to be, we are still required to operate based on the dominator's terms and play according to their rules. By being 'intersectional', minoritized subjects end up carrying a larger representation load and having to perform multiple identities and represent multiple minoritized communities at the diversity events. One respondent complained about the 'intersectional' labour involved:

> It just made me think about when we are being boxed this way. It seems that we have to carry many things … we have to worry as we do our job … we have to worry about how we are portraying to the white

> Australians … how we are betraying our communities to the white Australian people … how we are also portraying our communities to our own community people.

By allowing myself to be included in a wide range of diversity events for being the 'intersectional minority' poster child, I am aware that I am complicit in supporting the institution's whitewashing efforts. Bilge's (2014) words ring true:

> Whitening intersectionality does not refer to the race of intersectionality practitioners, but to the ways of doing intersectionality that rearticulate it around Eurocentric epistemologies. One does not need to be white to whiten intersectionality, as non-white and colonial immigrant scholars who are ideologically co-opted by dominant epistemologies also contribute to reproducing hegemonic knowledge. (2014: 190)

I have so often been recruited into superficial, tokenistic 'intersectional' efforts, and also willingly participate from time to time to display model minority citizenship, please white powers and appear less angry. I am cognizant that by agreeing to be the poster child, I too have colluded with white appropriations of intersectionality to 'normalise a race-optional, even race-free intersectionality' (Bilge 2014: 192), leave out truthful confrontations with extractive institutional conditions and structures that result in power differentials and, ultimately, conceal white supremacy and privilege. Bilge (2014) criticized that depoliticized intersectionality efforts deny, reduce and disassociate from race matters. What then do all these 'good will intersectional EDI initiatives' achieve if they continue to avoid tackling and whitewash away the real structural causes, reproduce hegemonies and maintain unequal power relations and systems? As Bilge (2014) concludes, they merely 'collude with neoliberal knowledge governance and the management of neutralised difference' (2014: 201).

There is indeed significant value in an intersectional feminist approach to do anti-coloniality, anti-racial capitalism and anti-patriarchy work, including reading, researching, listening, writing, teaching and resisting. The key is to counter depoliticized, identitarian intersectionality with relational intersectionality. Returning to Kimberle Crenshaw (1989) who coined the term 'intersectionality', her conceptualization emphasizes mutual constitution where complex interactions of systems of social relations come to produce different outcomes in specific historical and contemporary contexts. Yuval-Davis (2013) also clarifies that 'although discourses of race, gender, class, etc. have their own ontological bases which cannot be reduced to each other, there is no separate concrete meaning of any facet of these social categories, as they are mutually constitutive in any concrete historical moment' (2013: 7). By drawing attention to these works, I am not invested in what Jennifer Nash (2016) critiques about, the movement of 'intersectional originalism' where there has been a call for 'textual fidelity' to Crenshaw's original article and conceptualisation of intersectionality. My critiques of identitarian and corporatized intersectionality in the EDI space is not driven from a fidelity to the originators of intersectionality, desire to rescue intersectionality and maintain its 'purity' and 'originality' and exertion of territoriality in theorizing and practising intersectionality. Rather than joining faithful defenders of intersectionality's inaugural texts and going about to diagnose if intersectionality has been used as intended in Crenshaw's original article, I am more interested in exposing the corporatization of intersectionality for signalling 'diversity, inclusion and equity', maintaining white powers, enhancing corporate branding and ultimately monetary gains of the neoliberal university. I am invested in showing how the current myth of intersectionality in the EDI space gives a beautiful illusion that works are in progress to address inequalities and injustices. On the contrary, existing depoliticized, individualized, identity-focused and oppression-additive 'intersectional' efforts are evidently moving in a direction that buttress the colonial, white supremacist and neoliberal functions of the corporate university.

To counter that, I call for intersectional feminist approaches in the EDI space to be relational by considering unequal power relations constitutive of colonial histories and contemporary racial capitalist political and economic contexts, showing how such power structures work to produce privilege and oppression and affect lives in uneven and complex ways and making dominant white powers visible and accountable. A gender non-conforming presenting young woman respondent's sharing of her encounter with violence at her workplace raised important questions about employing a relational, intersectional approach to improving workplace safety:

> There was a physical attack at the school gate. A tall white man body slammed me. I felt very unsafe. Is it racism or sexism? Feel very unsafe. The impact is very great. This is the first time I met a direct attack. It really makes me very unsafe. With this incident, it made me even more careful and vigilant … It really affected me a lot and every time I walk along that road, I would be very affected … No point reporting. I don't have evidence I could present in the official complaint. No one will take me seriously. Who is this person? I am also aware of the backlash since everyone likes that person. No point racking it up and in the end I will face the backlash and no impact on the well liked white person.

When we consider the relational intersectionality of the broader forces behind this attack, we will appreciate the complex interrelatedness and entanglements of racism, heterosexism and xenophobia at work here. To meaningfully address workplace violence, we perhaps need to engage in uncomfortable interrogation of the intersection of whiteness, coloniality, white heteropatriarchy and racial capitalism in everyday life instead of hiding behind cosmetic display of additive victimhood caricatures.

Myth of diversity, inclusion and harmony

The theme for 2024 International Women's Day is Count Her In. It is not just that the pronoun, 'she/her' being used here to refer to women that is problematic in ways that immediately exclude non-binary and genderqueer women who may have preferred the pronoun 'they/them' to be used alongside. It also beckons the question of counting her in to do what and for who and whom. As a member of the campaign's target group, I do not want to be counted in for existing unequal structures that only continue to make dispossessed and disenfranchised peoples' everyday realities with white colonialism, racial capitalism, neoliberalism, heteropatriarchy and ableism challenging. I do not want to be counted in to reinforce the dominator's power, rules and logics and endorse my own and others' minoritization and oppression. I do not want to be counted in just because I will be rewarded with some scraps from the master's table having smiled enough and ticked the right boxes of approval. I do not want to be counted into something dirty like that. Writing about it already makes me want to take a shower. The theme, according to the International Women's Day webpage, is to inspire and invest in inclusion. Once again, inclusion or exclusion logic and representation politics loom over identity-driven campaigns like that. Identity-driven, inclusion-focused efforts not only assume their target group possesses essentialist, fixed and bounded identities and drive their initiatives based on certain assumptions of who their target group is but also reinforce the idea that their target group is standing outside, appealing to the goodness of the majority to be let in and allocated a share of the pie and will be grateful for the 'inclusion' and 'empowerment'. Undoubtedly, the rules have not changed no matter how sincere and successful these campaigns and initiatives are. The dominant racial capitalist, patriarchal and heteronormative landscape remains unshaken; the powerful stays powerful if not more powerful. If counting her in and being permitted to enter means that she is invited into a white colonial, racial capitalist, heteropatriarchal space and required to play by the rules set out for her by the white benevolent saviour-master, why would she want to be any part of this? Why would any woman or subjugated person want to be included based on those terms? Why would we want to enter such a game where we could not change the rules, have to play by dominator's rules and know that no matter how well we play the game in mimicking the master, the master continues to be powerful, and we remain less than equal and second-class?

Fundamentally, it is important to recognize that the inclusion/ exclusion mode of operation prevalent in the suite of diversity programmes for different target groups such as First Nations peoples, LGBTIQA+ individuals, women and culturally and linguistically diverse and marginalized communities are built on and continue to reinforce colonial and racial capitalist principles. The colonial rule of hierarchizing humanity and using such categorizing logic to justify colonisers' civilizing mission to dispossess Indigenous peoples, plunder native resources and control subjugated populations is not 'premised on a random pattern of intolerant behaviour but rather inscribed a systematic pattern of inclusion and exclusion' as Barry Morris (1989) pointed out (1989: 188). By subscribing to the inclusion/exclusion logic in the EDI space, various so-called inclusive efforts only reinforce the colonial logic of ranking humanity, deciding who gets to be included and how they will be included and dispersing resources based on their terms and threshold. In Aileen Moreton Robinson's (2020) critique of white feminism, she points out that 'offering to include is a sign of ownership and control, and inclusion of "Other" on white women's terms will not decentre white women's dominant status in Australian feminism' (2020: 62). This is an important critique that applies to the entire EDI space from gender equity to queer alliance to cultural diversity advocacy. Any diversity initiative designed on the premise of inclusion always already assumes a position of dominance, superiority and privilege. This systematic practice of inclusion is ultimately an expression of institutional and systemic racism that centres the dominator's power, ownership and control (Morris 1989).

The inclusion/exclusion logic often demands minoritized subjects prove their credentials to compete for inclusion and access. As evident in the whole suite of diversity programs with their awards, grants, scholarship and supportive initiatives, minoritized subjects must display model citizen's characteristics and a willingness to speak the dominator's lingo and stay within the borders defined for them to qualify for the prized and scarce resources the dominator has allocated to them. Having applied for some of these EDI awards and grants,

I attest to the hoops applicants must jump to put in a submission from writing pages of responses and evidence addressing the list of selection criteria to preparing presentations to attending interviews. Minoritized subjects when successful in their fight for resources against other minoritized subjects are then expected to and, in fact, groomed to display a sense of gratitude and recognition due to the prestige attached to the prized resources allocated by the dominator. Our 'diversity' faces are displayed across corporate promotional materials as the institution's prized show pony indicating the success of its EDI efforts. My affective response to being recognized and celebrated is one of happiness and pride. But deep down, I suspect others like me know we too are complicit in strengthening the unequal power structures that subjugate us in the first place.

In my earlier research on low-income marriage migrant women from less wealthy countries in the Southeast Asian region (Quah 2020a), I abhor the 'victim vs agent' binary discourse confining women from less wealthy countries in the binary categories of a pitiful victim and an empowered agent categories. The women either elicit sympathy from guilt-conscious wealthier subjects in more powerful countries who proclaim, 'these women are really pitiful, we must save them' or are recognized and included for their neoliberal, (re)productive potential and model minority attributes – 'they are just like us, they are good people too'. This pernicious binary narrows attention to individual identity and behaviour demanding subjects to perform the role of victim or agent and prove their eligibility accordingly for scraps from the master's table. Such an approach in politics, policy and services does not do anything to flip and thrash the master's table! It only skirts around the root cause. Subordinated minions will only continue to dance around the table in hope of the master's attention and recognition. 'Look at me, look at me! I am worthy!' While minoritized populations struggle for recognition and inclusion in mainstream society, fighting for scraps from the master's table, the master continues their domination and maintains their power (Puar 2017). As Lorde (2019) said, 'the master's tools will never dismantle the master's house'

(2019: 103), the multibillion-dollar industries of corporate diversity and inclusion and health and well-being ultimately will not dismantle racial capitalist and neoliberal structures and achieve social justice and equity. On the contrary, these are the master's tools that will only enrich the master and their empire. Far too often, even passionate activists and well-meaning community workers unfortunately get caught up in the struggles for identity and representation politics and unknowingly end up policing identity borders and reinforcing colonial constructions and hierarchical categorizations of race, gender and sexuality. As long as we are busy classifying people and striving in our activism to 'include' and 'represent' those who have been disenfranchised by the dominant culture, we are bound to reinforce existing systems of hegemony, leaving some out and further alienating others. Expectedly, the existing colonial, racial capitalist, neoliberal and heteropatriarchal power systems responsible for the unequal distribution of life chances do not get dismantled, and deeply embedded unjust power relations remain intact if not stronger.

When the solution to structural inequalities becomes reduced to a sneaky smokescreen of multiculturalism, diversity and inclusion, we assume unequal power relations would be abolished if only we could recognize, include and celebrate more diverse categories of identities.

Several respondents that I spoke with observe that contrary to their proclaimed aims, these corporate branding programmes, more often than not, create decoys to deflect attention from the majority's excessive powers and the persistent unequal relations between power holders and minoritized peoples and communities. One respondent lamented over the hollowness, superficiality and tokenism of corporate EDI efforts at the university and how such efforts seek to create the myth of diversity and inclusion without the intent to question privilege and power hoarding:

> I mean, there's so much effort around, you know equity and diversity.
> I mean, the University is doing so much to gesture to all these things
> somewhat seriously. There is a lot of like gesturing and posturing,

but a lot of it feels like it's very empty. I don't know if the University's any worse or better than a lot of workplaces except it should know better, I think academia should be held to a higher standard. I think it's fundamentally that people being uncomfortable and unwilling to question their own advantage, and the ways that they might contribute to a racist work environment. Because no one likes to admit that. So that's why I think universities go for diversity and inclusion, and that really bothers me, the language. And the measures, they are all woman fuzzy, but not many universities explicitly push an anti-racist agenda. And I think that's why racism persists because you don't counter racism with diversity and inclusion, you counter it with anti-racism, and that's a different set of measures.

It is therefore no surprise that some of the respondents who work in the EDI space bemoan over having to consider senior executive leaders' 'threshold' and 'appetite' in making meaningful changes in policy and practice. To have to consider senior executives' 'threshold' and 'appetite' seems to suggest that there is institutional resistance all the way to the top level of power holders to exercise political will in instating social justice principles, disrupting unequal power relations and interrogating unjust power structures that perpetuate the problems of marginalization EDI efforts claim to address. The empirical data suggests that EDI programmes are more eager to keep the status quo and 'peace and harmony' rather than interrogate and dismantle unjust structures. One respondent exposed such institutional resistance where universities' EDI gestures lack political courage to shake things up and topple existing unequal power hierarchy:

> It's all white men at the top with a couple of white women sprinkled in there for fun … they just pretend they're in the right … the gender equity awards … they just pretend, and then they want to control it all … it just seems like smoke and mirrors … they act like they're doing something, but they really don't want to do anything.

Another respondent also criticized the superficial, essentialist treatment of culture in cultural awareness and competency programs and lamented that even such careful EDI initiatives that did not wish to rock the boat for the majority were still enough to rouse the displeasure of the white faculty:

> I'm sorry I'm laughing, because it's just literally, two years ago they mandated cultural competency for the entire workforce … the way my white colleagues reacted, the amount of resistance and aggression was created as a result … And that training is so weak, it's touched thin in culture and I hate the language of competency, it's deeply problematic …What anti-racist diversity could look like right instead of this liberal 'let's just celebrate some holidays, and otherwise pretend we don't see color and race' thing … superficial multiculturalism, this refusal to deal with the diversity of the pluralism within each of our communities … I don't' know if it is convenient or wilful ignorance.

Cultural diversity celebratory events such as Harmony Day framed as promoting community building, multiculturalism, intercultural and inter-faith understanding are sold as an antidote to racism, prejudice, extremism and violence. Ironically, Harmony Day instated in 1999 used to encourage intercultural understanding and harmonious coexistence in the Australian society and persistently celebrated in schools and universities has deep-seated colonial violent roots (Australian Human Rights Commission 2023). Instead of honouring United Nations' International Day for the Elimination of Racial Discrimination on 21 March, Australia sneakily rebranded it with Harmony Day shifting the focus from solidarity with people struggling with systemic racism to harmony celebrations where individuals and communities come together to sweep racism under the rug and deny the presence of racism (Australian Human Rights Commission 2023). Indigenous peoples in Australia have long protested against the celebration of Harmony Day since Harmony Day officiates Australia's insistent refusal to condemn Sharpeville massacre in South Africa in 1960 in the same vein as their refusal to acknowledge and condemn earlier massacres of Aboriginal peoples in Australia (Pearson 2023). Schools, universities and workplaces around Australia celebrate Harmony Day 'pretending that we have racial "harmony" by ignoring the voices of the oppressed and Australia's long history of oppression, where our own racist laws paved the way to apartheid' (Pearson 2023). As Gamilaroi man and founder of IndigenousX, Luke Pearson's strongly worded indictment indicates, 'Harmony Day is not just a distraction from the work of eliminating racism, it is an active argument against it … Harmony Day posits a world where there is no racism to eradicate, so all we need to do is pat ourselves on the back for being so multicultural and bring in a plate of food to have a nice morning tea'(Pearson 2023). These cultural diversity celebration events paper over systemic colonial violence and racism and create a veneer of harmony pretending that progress and equity have been achieved and coloniality and racism have come to pass.

Myth of complaint and redress avenues

Clearly, the function of EDI in corporations, including the university, first and foremost works to support the business model of these entities and if that means maintaining status quo, keeping the peace and harmony and ensuring subordinated subjects stay quiet, subservient and grateful, that will be done. This study's empirical evidence and critiques of EDI programmes (for example, Collins 2011; Ahmed 2012) point to the corporate tactic of using the language of diversity and inclusion to present a harmonious picture of empowered minorities of diverse backgrounds. This shiny corporate poster splashed across billboards and social media feeds not only creates the myth that we have done enough to diversify, include and improve access, which helps power holders sleep better but also sells to subordinated peoples the myth that the society has come a long way and in fact arrived at a more equitable and just place for minorities. These programs drive home a propaganda that the society has done well and proven their capabilities of overcoming disharmonies, as long as we continue to lock arms and work hard to protect the earned harmony. Such relentless efforts in pushing forth this happy family picture are good for business, generate profits for those in power and bring dividends to those who assimilate. They do hardly anything to tip the scale of powers and resources to improve minoritized subjects' everyday realities embedded within dominant structures. The success and effectiveness of these corporate branding efforts lie in maintaining the myths of progress and harmony where we have evolved into better human beings who care about the less advantaged and powerful, and we ought to congratulate ourselves for coming this far with all the diversity and inclusion awards we have bagged.

What is really at stake in this EDI circus is 'whether whites' monopoly over socio-economic power and privilege, and the underlying ideology that supports this position, will be sustained. Or, conversely, whether positions of power and privilege will be reapportioned to let non-whites in' (Collins 2011: 519). At the point of writing this book, media articles on the resignation of John Hopkins Medicine's Chief Diversity Officer due to backlash on her email on privilege caught my attention (Afro News 2024; Baltimore Fishbowl 2024; New York Post 2024). Dr Sherita Golden was pressured to resign after receiving online attacks by anti-wokeness, right-wing conservatives, politicians and uber-rich capitalists. The latter branded her article as racist and a diversity hit list since she has had the audacity to call out white men as having unearned privileges. In her monthly diversity digest article, she provided a textbook definition of privilege – 'a set of unearned benefits given to people who are in a specific social group. Privilege operates on personal, interpersonal, cultural and institutional levels, and it provides advantages and favors to members of dominant groups at the expense of members of other groups' and named 'white people, able-bodied people, heterosexuals, cisgender people, males, Christians, middle or owning class people, middle-aged people and English-speaking people' as examples of privilege groups in the white American society (Afro News 2024; Baltimore Fishbowl 2024; New York Post 2024). She explained further in her article the workings of privilege where 'people in dominant groups often believe they have earned the privileges they enjoy or that everyone could have access to these privileges if only they worked to earn them. In fact, privileges are unearned and granted to people in the dominant groups whether they want those privileges or not, and regardless of their stated intent' (Afro News 2024; Baltimore Fishbowl 2024; New York Post 2024). A standard definition of privilege that many race, gender and sexuality teachers would teach in class has landed John Hopkins Medicine's Chief Diversity Officer in hot soup. To do diversity, inclusion and equity according to social justice principles, she did the right thing by discussing the concept of privilege. But even her straightforward, textbook explanation of privilege proved to be too radical and uncomfortable for the privileged and powerful, who would do anything it takes to secure what they have hoarded. Golden's diversity digest article stating the obvious about privilege expectedly received attacks from those who perceive such calling out and provocation as threatening to their privileged positions. Unfortunately, she had to concede defeat, retract her definition of privilege, apologize for her article which she called it 'poorly worded' and resign from the position (Afro News 2024; Baltimore Fishbowl 2024; New York Post 2024). Perhaps having let in and enjoyed power and privileges reapportioned to her, it would be understandably hard to stand by her original position to expose privilege and demand redress. Executive leaders from John Hopkins University's Faculty of Medicine, while accepting her resignation under such circumstances, emphasized their commitment to 'address health disparities and increase retention and recruitment of diverse talent, all in service of the richly diverse communities we serve' (Afro News 2024; Baltimore Fishbowl 2024; New York Post 2024). These words seem to ring hollow when they bowed to pressures by the rich and powerful who refuse to acknowledge their privileges, let alone give up their privileges, and in the end, let go of a minority staff who dared to tell the truth about the role of power and privilege in causing disparities and injustices. In a perverse way, calling out white privilege becomes framed as racist and divisive. One cannot help but wonder about the definitions of inclusion and diversity and the use of EDI program in corporate settings. When EDI workers and minoritized subjects like Golden seek to address inequalities, inequities, disparities and injustices, the language of inclusion and diversity is in turn weaponized by the privileged majority and power holders to accuse them of being divisive, disruptive and even racist. It is hard not to get a sense that the function of EDI is merely cosmetic and aesthetic, and its purpose is to create a façade of diversity and harmony for sustaining white powers' ownership and control of socio-economic benefits.

In a similar vein, some of my respondents' and my personal encounters in Australian universities also show how those who told the truths about colonialism, racial capitalism, white supremacy and privilege inevitably faced punishment for disrupting the harmony orchestrated by dominant powers. A few respondents having written and published research articles on racism and using auto-ethnographical and qualitative interview data to substantiate their rigorous research on racism at the workplace in Australian universities reported enduring serious backlash. Perceived as troublemakers and traitors of the organization, we became the target of aggressive campaigns where the whole suite of bureaucratic mechanisms was used to put us in our place for complaining, protesting and speaking up. We experienced the fullness of institutional force through the university's execution and threats of disciplinary measures. One respondent confided:

> My worst fear emerged about three months after I wrote about racism … when we did my annual performance review, I published a lot of papers, but all of that was ignored, and she said, because I published that one article, it besmirched the reputation of the university, and so she rated me underperforming on research purely on that basis. And this was just so weird. I said that to the union this shouldn't have happened like this makes no sense … from the union's perspective, unless she's firing you, and you've got an unfair dismissal case, you know that she can kind of write whatever she wants in your performance review. But it did have enormous impact on that. I wasn't eligible for any bonus pay because of that evaluation and it also caused me a lot of anxiety and a lot of worry over that period. And then, consistently for the three years after that, she found something to write me as underperforming.

Another account revealed the disciplinary measures used against protesters of institutional racism:

> The crazy thing is that after writing about institutional racism, not only did I not get any support from my university, I received a grievance complaint complaining that I damaged the university's reputation and the reputation of the racists I wrote about. The 'good' white woman managers hauled me in for investigation meeting, put me on a gag order, threatened with termination of employment if I breach gag order during investigation. I was slapped with reminders of staff's code of conduct and respect for diversity clauses and then a list of remedial actions to appease the complainer. Ironic that when a woman of colour complained about whiteness, she was reminded to be respectful of diversity.

The intention of these elaborate, behind-closed-doors moves was to break the minoritized protester, and the institution certainly succeeded in debilitating and injuring the protester for having the audacity to point out the obvious – white powers and their racial privilege. Some of the women in the sample reported significant negative outcomes after encountering punitive measures and they range from job loss to halt of career progression to financial challenges to breakdown of social relationships to health issues such as complex post-traumatic stress disorder, depression, anxiety disorder, fibromyalgia and, sadly, even terminal illnesses.

A few respondents that I spoke with revealed that they turned to the university's complaint mechanism to lodge their own complaints against racism and related discriminatory treatments. However, they soon found out that the official complaint mechanism was not meant for minoritized staff members to protest against institutional racism and seek redress. Sara Ahmed's (2021) research on *Complaint!* examines the oppressive, silencing and overall futile process of engaging with the university's official complaint mechanism by following the accounts of forty students, academics, researchers and administrators who have used the mechanism to register their complaints. Ahmed (2021) shows how the official complaint mechanism is meant to discourage complaints, weaken the complainer, erode hopes for redress and rectification and promote fatalism where one no longer believes that unjust systems and practices can be made right ever. In line with Ahmed's research findings, this study's empirical evidence points to the complainer incurring greater injury from the act of complaining than from the earlier act of racial aggression they have encountered. It is as if when one complains, one is banging one's head against the wall and ends up with a bloodied head from the relentless banging where the wall remains unscratched and solid. It is no wonder that several respondents of this study resigned to the fact that there were no meaningful and real avenue of seeking redress. The process of proving to white powers that they have suffered racism has proven to be daunting enough:

> How do you prove that there's this certain type of thinking or attitude … or so it's really your opinion that you're putting forward … maybe you could raise a complaint formally with an institution or with university but these things … they are just very difficult as you would know.

The women respondents did not think they would be believed and obtain reparative justice.

Worse, white people are often called to be the arbitrator of justice in these complaints of racism. Ironically, they get to decide if there is indeed a case of racism or if complaints are groundless and should thereby be dismissed.

A respondent described her experience when she lodged a formal complaint of the racist treatment she received from a white woman colleague:

> Throughout the complaint management process, the case investigator would repeatedly use guiding language to tell me that this is cultural difference, not racism. They would say Australians tend to use English to make jokes, tend to be very direct, this is just a cultural difference, they don't mean it. They keep trying to diminish racism

and point to cultural difference and my lack of understanding that it is cultural difference. I did not think it was cultural clash. It was clearly racism and I used the word racism in my complaint … There was no resolution provided by the complaint management unit. She resigned in the end and the complaint management unit officer also resigned so there was no follow up … Though I did not win, I needed to make a stand when necessary so that the people after me would not have to suffer like that.

The complaint management system has proven to be yet another institutional tool to protect white powers instead of addressing redress. While the institution proclaims to take complaints of racism and any form of discrimination seriously, the experiences of respondents who have used the official complaint mechanism point to how the white people complaint handlers were eager to minimize or dismiss racism complaints. When a respondent complained about institutional racism using the official complaint mechanism, the complaint handler referred their case to the human resource department instead of an independent entity in handling racial discrimination and workplace health and safety. When asked why that was the case, the complaint handler explained almost indignantly that their case was now under the purview of the human resource department because they have involved the union in their representation. Their case was eventually dismissed by the human resource department as having found no case of racism. Once again, white powers arbitrate and rule that there is no racism even though racialized subjects protest and complain. Perversely, the complaint management system is often weaponized by privileged people to cry grievance over perceived threat to destabilize their privileges and powers. In one of the above examples, white privileged people used the complaint management system to lodge grievance complaints when they feel wrongfully accused of racism or aggrieved for reputational damages from being accused of racism. The complaint management system turns out to an institutional tool to protect the interests of dominant powers and maintain the myths of harmony they have created.

Myth of individual responsibility and allyship

From Harmony Day to Mardi Gras Pride Parade to RUOK Day to Consent Matters to RespectNow, the modus operandi has been based on an individualistic approach focusing on personal identity, morality, behaviour, agency and responsibility. A casual review of Australian universities' EDI webpages shows a mirror image of American and British universities' EDI webpages with a generous platter of resources, guides, instructions and learning modules prompting staff to better themselves as an ally, bystander, first respondent and co-worker. For example, universities with anti-racism or cultural competence webpages list resources heavily dependent on self-improvement, self-development and self-help where individual staff are expected to work on their identities, attitudes, values, behaviours, relationships and prejudices to prevent racism and build a collegial and harmonious work environment. A short half-minute video clip titled, 'Elevator – Racism. It stops with me' by the Australian Human Rights Commission could be commonly spotted on universities' anti-racism webpages. The clip features an elevator incident where a visibly white man holds the elevator for a flustered visibly white woman and, like a gentleman, invites her to enter the elevator first before him. However, when he sees a visibly black or brown woman of colour run towards the elevator, he steps into the elevator right away and attempts to close the elevator door in her face. The white woman annoyed with his behaviour steps out of the elevator, stands by the woman of colour and both women give the white man a hard glare. The woman of colour is visibly pleased that the white woman stands up for her and by her. The clip ends with a message, 'Racism. It stops with me'. This clip accompanies online learning modules, reading materials and research reports on bystander anti-racism initiatives urging individual staff to be an active anti-racism bystander standing up and speaking out for victims of racism when they witness the incident. Since the message emphasizes that racism stops with me, the onus is on me to stop racism from happening. Incredibly,

I possess the power to stop racism. I wish I have the supernatural powers to stop racism.

Another anti-racism video produced by an Australian mental health organization to promote self-regulated, anti-prejudice attitude and behaviour is also ubiquitously found on Australian universities' EDI webpages. The one-minute video on the invisible discriminator displaying casual racist behaviours including refusing to sit close to or next to an Indigenous person or person of colour in public spaces and on public transportation, watching them suspiciously in a convenience shop and making racist jokes about them in a bar. The video ends with a message: 'Discrimination leads to depression and anxiety in Indigenous Australians. No one should be made to feel like crap just for being who they are. You can change this.' This video perpetuates victimhood of minoritized Indigenous Australian subjects and appeals to the sympathy and benevolence of the non-Indigenous audience. It reduces ongoing dispossession and racialized violence of colonialism in Indigenous Australians' lives to a simple matter of individual non-Indigenous people's discriminatory attitudes against Indigenous Australians. It places the responsibility of addressing racial injustice Indigenous Australians are subjected to on non-Indigenous individuals and absolves colonial institutions' culpability. A whole range of bystander anti-racism programs and resources from Everyday Racism app to 'What to do if you witness racism on the bus' guide emphasizing personal civic responsibility in preventing racism through mutual surveillance and discipline is also provided on the universities' anti-racism webpages. One could also learn how to be an anti-racism bystander by watching a series of educational videos explaining what bystanders need to do in various racist scenarios in public spaces such as the train, shopping mall, sporting event and internet. Be it bystander programme for anti-racism, anti-sexual violence or anti-queerphobia, as Nash (2019b) indicates, 'the logic of bystander program is that everyone is a witness to potential violence, and thus everyone should be enlisted in labouring to "prevent" or eliminate violence' (2019b: 206). In bystander programmes, individual staff or citizen is evidently tasked with the responsibility to fix problems that are fundamentally historical, structural and institutional.

This created myth of how every individual member of the organization is equally responsible for the overall safety and well-being of the workplace and that the goodness, agency and courage of individuals are all that is needed to fix structural and institutional problems is extremely persuasive and convincing with repeated indoctrination by the full corporate suite of EDI and other human resource management and organization development programmes. From time to time, the university would engage paid external trainers and consultants to train their staff members in these EDI areas, hence contributing to the notion that individual staff members could do better and ought to be trained to be a more active ally and bystander, and that the problem lies with individual attitudes and behaviours and as long as those are fixed, the problem will be solved. Whether it's consent matters sex education modules, sexual harassment and sexual assault prevention programme, anti-racism project, LGBTIQA+ ally training, cultural awareness training and cultural diversity celebrations, the business model is driven by an individualist approach where the responsibility to manage risk of violence, police deviance and threats of safety and create a harmonious and safe work environment lies with individual staff members. Responsibilizing the self, as scholars (Besley & Peters 2007; Peters 2007; Nash 2019b) have pointed out, is a feature of neoliberalism where individuals are called to be a 'moral agent' and 'calculative rational choice actor' (Peters 2007: 92) expected to deploy 'managerial, economic and actuarial techniques to themselves' (Besley & Peters 2007: 172) in every decision concerning their bodies, education, employment, relationship arrangements, health and retirement. The EDI programmes emphasizing individual responsibility, self-regulation and personal agency is undoubtedly a neoliberal tool to self-manage risks, deflect attention from extractive work conditions the institution creates, blunt employees' class consciousness, disavow institutional responsibilities and enhance business performance.

It is not just EDI programmes where neoliberal logic is applied. One other popular individual-focused corporate tactic to deflect attention from institutional responsibility in creating exploitative work conditions is staff health and well-being. Both areas are under the purview of human resource management, and the latter's existence is always first and foremost to safeguard the employer's and institution's financial interests by managing employees in ways that enhance their productivity and remove obstacles that affect workers' performance. The goal is fundamentally, optimization or exploitation of labour and maximization or plundering of profits. One may argue that human resource employees working in these units are well-meaning and sincere in caring about equity, diversity, inclusion and well-being. However, their misplaced kindness and compassion unfortunately only make them a highly efficient and complicit cog in the neoliberal machine. At the point of writing this section, I was down with Covid-19. At least one-third of the attendees were infected with Covid-19 after attending a four-hour, in-person meeting in a crowded and poorly ventilated seminar room. What was even more amusing in hindsight about this Covid-19 super spreader meeting was that an external consultant was hired to conduct a one-hour self-care and wellbeing session. The staff meeting emphasziing self-care and well-being ironically turned out to be a Covid-19 super spreader event that consequently caused harm to staff's health and well-being! The white woman consultant in her eagerness to get through to the packed room of highly educated academic and professional employees gifted us with a simple self-care formula, S.N.A.P. to improve personal wellbeing and drive all our oppressions away. S.N.A.P. stands for 'S', soothing touch, 'N', name the emotion, 'A', act, and 'P', praise'. The message was clear: you cannot change the structures and your environments, but you can acknowledge your emotions and change your mindset. Once again, another tired corporate tactic aimed to deflect attention from institutional roles in perpetuating deep-rooted and serious structural issues at the workplace and shift the responsibility of making the workplace safe and healthy to worn-out employees themselves. Held captive to the business pitch of this external consultancy company, we did our best to be kind to the external speaker, sat through it all and engaged in the planned activities like good, obedient corporate citizens. Instead of turning to experts within the university, universities often expend funds to engage external consultants and contribute to the professionalization of EDI sector. In fact, several Australian universities are also offering EDI and staff well-being graduate programmes to create a professional class of EDI experts to advise corporations' EDI and staff well-being initiatives. Instead of considering carefully how they may use their power and resources to reject neoliberal, extractive logic that is ultimately responsible for perpetuating work conditions that compromise staff's health and wellbeing, institutions aided by eager executives shift the spotlight to individual staff members' personal responsibility in practising self-care, naming their anger and frustration, letting negative emotions go and keeping a gratitude journal.

As evidenced, attribution of personal responsibility in the EDI space is disproportionate and misplaced. For individual staff members who identify possessing privileges in one or multiple ways, they are expected to undergo various unconscious bias, bystander and ally training programmes and be a kinder, more compassionate, empathetic, not racist, Indigenous-supportive, LGBTIQA+ friendly and pro-gender equity-cisgender heterosexual women employee. It is not uncommon to witness bragging of EDI credentials in email signatures, workplace conversations and official newsletters as if these EDI certificates, awards and badges possess whitewashing magical powers that have turned participants into a 'I am not racist, sexist, homophobic' person. For minoritized subjects, it means additional workload they have to carry and extra labour they end up performing in EDI spaces supposedly created to support them. They are expected to subscribe to self-improvement training and leadership development programmes to be empowered, display more confidence and courage, lean in, fight to be included and have their voice heard. They are also often tasked with the responsibility to be the spokesperson and represent minority voices. One respondent who worked in the EDI space complained to me that being categorized as culturally diverse, shorthand for non-Anglo white, she has been delegated with every EDI work that has to do with cultural diversity:

> They'll say we need to put more people of diverse cultural backgrounds in leadership. And I'm like cool. And then they'll look at me and I'll be like why is this my problem? Just because I'm the only person of a different background, so to say. Why is it suddenly my thing to have to be responsible for? They feel that they can't do anything about it, like oh, I don't have a diverse cultural background so it is her problem. So it almost feels to me it's a bit of a redundant conversation … The top is a white man, right? … The rest are all white women … they're not necessarily responsible, or they don't feel attached, they don't necessarily see what kind of impact it will have on people. I find that really ironic because they're supposed to be intelligent people.

Minoritized subjects are not only expected to overcome their marginalization, emerge 'confident and empowered', never show any vulnerability and lean in to align with white powers, they are also expected to labour for the institution's whitewashing campaigns which are purportedly sold as beneficial to marginalized peoples. One respondent laughed in reflection of the EDI efforts at their workplace:

> Look at the people who are doing the EDI work. It is all the minorities doing the EDI work. Isn't it very laughable and ridiculous? Don't you think it is really funny?

Hirshfield & Joseph (2012) calls this 'identity taxation', where staff identified with possessing marginalized social identities in demographic categories such as gender, sexual orientation and race end up doing additional service work in the university. Individual minoritized subjects enter each of the institution's EDI spaces and end up doing the diversity work, performing emotional labour as poster children, expending already limited resources and being further debilitated. In these factory spaces, their marginalized experiences are transformed into a product that the neoliberal employer could use to sell their brand, and the minoritized communities they help form and maintain serves to contain grievances and keep false hopes up. This approach in the EDI space like other functions in the university 'borrows from a set of discourses and practices that 'elide the structuring violences of neoliberal governance and capital in favour of a liberal ideal that celebrates individuality as personal responsibility, but also employability' (Kwon & Nguyen 2016). It turns employees into consumer-capitalist subjects motivating and incentivizing them to move towards individual consumption of the platter of self-making empowerment products and produce charitable service for one another. When promotion applications now require employees to demonstrate how they have supported EDI principles, their participation in the EDI circus will only enhance their employability and career progression. The individualistic approach not only places too much pressure and too heavy of a responsibility on individual staff to address problems that are fundamentally structural and systemic but also deepens a binary narrative and deficit culture of victimhood versus agency and oppression versus saviourhood. More seriously, it once again distracts us from holding broader structures and institutions accountable for their culpability, complicity and responsibilities and channelling our resources to dismantling these unjust systems and building more sustainable and just structures and futures.

It is the same with celebrations of cultural diversity that shift focus from structural and systemic racism to individual learning and celebration of multiple, diverse cultures. Without interrogating historical, inherited and interrelated asymmetrical power relations and structures, the efforts and resources invested in them, no matter how well-meaning and sincere these cultural diversity celebrations aim to be, will only reinforce the dominance and privileges of power holders. They continually cover up root problems and focus their energies and resources on not just individualizing the problems but also shifting the responsibility of maintaining status quo of white dominance to individuals and often already minoritized, racialized subjects. The elaborate posturing of cultural diversity impose on individual racialized subjects the emotional, cultural and colonial labour of teaching white majority about their cultures and often end up exoticizing, racializing and orientalizing their cultural heritage to satisfy the white gaze (Quah & Tang 2024). Instead of attacking dominant power structures that result in the contemporary problems of inequalities, violence and injustices the world is plagued with, we busy ourselves with individual identity markers, inclusion efforts, diversity celebrations and ally training that do nothing to dismantle unjust hierarchal structures, reorganize relations and improve equitable access to life chances and safety. More often than not, these goodwill EDI gestures remain tokenistic and deflect attention from systemic issues resulting in racism, sexism, queerphobia, poor health outcomes and a low if not hazardous level of workplace health and safety. The everyday realities against inequalities and injustice persist for peoples oppressed in different, multiple and complex ways, and white powers persist in being invisible and dominant.

Minoritized subjects are not absolved from culpability and complicity in maintaining these myths of diversity, inclusion and harmony and aiding the neoliberal university function and prosper. From time to time, as a salaried employee of the institution, I perform the role of a poster child, walk with the university's float in the pride parade, join a gender equity working party, attend office's Lunar New Year morning tea and participate in marketing events to sell the university's brand and impress as a good citizen. From time to time, I speak the right corporate lingo so that I will be seen by our superiors and co-workers as a grateful, cooperative, positive and not angry employee ready to apply for promotion. From time to time, I get tired of complaining and being burnt out from the backlash, decide to pick my battles out of self-protection and self-preservation and, as a result, let the ball drop in my abolitionist feminist missions against ongoing colonialism, racial capitalism and neoliberalism at the workplace. The toss and turn between corporate citizenship and abolition feminism is a hard space to navigate especially when we receive a salary and are required to carry out work duties outlined in our work contract, some of which certainly bolster the neoliberal functions of the institution but contravene our feminist ethics. By playing the master's game and consenting to being co-opted in our own and others oppression, we become an accomplice complicit in enhancing colonial, racial capitalist, white patriarchal logics.

Co-workers who have been marginalized in some forms including white women, men of colour, women of colour and queer folks have proclaimed to me that they want to take up leadership positions and are determined to make positive changes from within. Some are optimistic that their clever and careful efforts in strategizing, sneaking in structural changes, speaking the correct lingo and getting buy-in from particular executive leaders they are aligned with are the ways in which they can meaningfully address inequity at the workplace. While they sign up for equity and diversity working committees and get involved in institutional branding exercises including EDI awards like Science in Australia Gender Equity (SAGE) and Australian Workplace Equity Index (AWEI), they believe they could move beyond tick-box, self-congratulatory gestures to actual cultural and policy shift. A respondent expressed her aspirations:

> I was seriously considering resigning, but there was no guarantee if I moved to another university … this senior academic told me if I go, then it's giving them victory. She told me to stick around. And there is the diversity and inclusion campaign that need us. They need our face, our yellow face now and then for their campaigns. She said, in five to ten years there'll be more Asian women in academics, so her advice is, stick around, be a pain in their ass. Speak up your mind. I think she is right. I'm determined to stick around and be a pain in the ass and join the senior management. Quitting is definitely giving them the victory. You and I, and all other Asian female academics stay in our position, move up, go for promotion. Be in the promotion and recruitment committees. I think that's the way to go. I can't see any other way to beat this. If we tolerate them, they will go bigger, and they won't regret. They will still see us as someone they can squash, step over us and injure us.

While their intentions are not in the wrong place, I worry about the effectiveness of their strategies that are ultimately individualized efforts playing safe by the master's rule book. I ask how we may strategically disrupt unjust power relations if we enrol ourselves into leadership positions of existing dominant, normative structures operating on colonial, racial capitalist, neoliberal and heteropatriarchal logics that require us to emulate the image of white, elite, cisgender, heterosexual man and regard the latter as success benchmark. Once we are permitted to enter and take a seat at the leadership table, are we able to change the rules since we have already taken the carrot that was previously dangling in front of us? The difficulty lies in guarding ourselves from being co-opted and used as diversity, inclusion and harmony signpost for the gratification of white powers. The worry is how well-meaning, passionate marginalized people and self-proclaimed allies may end up expending finite energy and resources and suffering a burn-out, or succumbing to co-optation and ultimately empowering and enriching the very power structures they seek to dismantle.

Coda: Anti-racist and anti-colonial critiques of EDI not the same as right-wing capitalists' calls for divestment in 'wokeness'

While I join anti-racist, anti-colonial, queer, intersectional and transnational feminists to critique the neoliberal and whitewashing logics of corporate EDI programmes, I am cognizant of how our critiques may unintentionally be weaponized as ammunitions for right-wing conservatives and capitalist executives, entrepreneurs and bureaucrats to pursue their white supremacist and profit-obsessed projects. The latter have been demanding the divestment and closure of EDI departments and arguing that 'wokeness' has gone overboard. For example, the University of Florida in the United States of America closed down its EDI office and thirteen full-time employees and fifteen administrative appointees lost their job consequently (Diverse 2024). Florida's governor who led the attack on EDI claimed victory, 'DEI is toxic and has no place in our public universities. I'm glad that Florida was the first state to eliminate DEI and I hope more states follow suit'

(Diverse 2024). The Florida state governor closed all EDI offices in the whole state for their perceived wokeness (Diverse 2024). Other US states such as Oklahoma and Texas follow suit in defunding and banning EDI programmes. Besides politicians, prominent white billionaire corporate honchos also attack EDI programs as woke-washing, anti-white people, reverse racist, money-wasting corporate functions and are eager to shut them down and cut costs. Consequently, EDI scholars, practitioners and consultants – the service subcontractors fuelling the multi-billion-dollar global EDI industrial complex – have come forward to defend EDI. This attack and defence of EDI could be observed here in the Australian higher education landscape where EDI offices are often at risk of removal during organization restructure. EDI units are often perceived as 'feel-good', staff welfare add-ons that are good for staff morale and community building, which translates into capital and complements neoliberal projects. Since EDI units are seen as frivolous, good-to-have add-ons, they are more likely to face the axe whenever there is an organization restructure resulting from economic anxieties about government funding cuts and decrease in student enrolments and thereby possible financial crisis. My critiques here on the myths of EDI do not belong to either camp – the anti-wokeness, white supremacist, capitalist attackers of EDI on the one hand and, on the other hand, the defenders' camp comprising monied EDI experts and consultants who are oftentimes minoritized consumer-capitalist subjects co-opted for neoliberal projects rather than working for political, social justice activisms. My critiques are not to be weaponized as ammunitions by the first camp for their white supremacist and neoliberal agendas. Neither should my critiques make me an enemy of the EDI defenders camp. It is precisely my opposition of white supremacy, racial capitalism and neoliberalism that I critique the existing corporate model of EDI as enabling the status quo preservation of unequal power structures. The proliferation and normalization of ostentatious bragging of inclusion and diversity in corporate sectors including higher education industry have gained significant successes in deflecting attention from ongoing and escalating coloniality, racial capitalism, neoliberalism and institutional and casual racisms at the workplace. Instead of moving restrictively and gingerly within the confines of existing neoliberal model of EDI, I am demanding for more. I am not contented with staying within the borders and attempting to revamp from within, where I reckon such futile and self-depleting efforts a shameful waste of finite feminist resources and energies. I am asking for an anti-colonial, anti-racial capitalist, intersectional feminist approach to social justice work that is not content with representation and identity politics, does not turn a blind eye or pay lip service to the dominance of white supremacist, colonial, racial capitalist, neoliberal and patriarchal regimes and will not gaslight marginalized peoples with 'things are better now' and 'things will get better' corporate nonsense.

5

Conclusion: Fire dragon feminist hopes and strategies

In a podcast episode, Saidiya Hartman spoke that the need to explain and provide explanations accompanying narratives and empirical data was a colonial politics and practice. She attempted to break free of the colonial imposition of explanation in her writing of *Wayward Lives, Beautiful Experiments* (Hartman 2019):

> I'm friends with the poet Dionne Brand, and we have this running discussion about narrative, and she always says 'Ah, too much explanation, too much explanation'. And for her there's a certain kind of politics of explanation that's all about coloniality, what are we explaining to whom? So, I think that my aim in *Wayward Lives*, and just generally in the work, is to become freer and freer, and really to let go some of that training, to let go certain modes of scholarly argumentation and evidence. I make a kind of compromise in *Wayward Lives*. (Hartman 2022)

Throughout the earlier chapters of the book, I have provided theoretical analyses and scholarly explanations while attempting to foreground the women's stories and experiences and engage in collaborative storytelling, thinking and writing alongside the women as much as I could. In this final chapter, I respond to Hartman's (2022) reflection on the coloniality of explanations and be 'freer and freer' in presenting the women's fiery hopes, moving poetry, fearless activisms and inspirational achievements. Instead of theorizing and explaining any further, the book's concluding notes centre the women's feminist hopes and tactics from a racialized Asian migrant woman's perspective. This book has attempted to collect, document and archive valuable and important stories of Asian migrant women's racialized existence and unrelenting, gnawing and undignified experiences with racial violence of different sorts, in particular, within the contexts of Australian academy and white settler-colonial society. In addition, the project also asks after the women's anti-colonial and anti-racist feminist strategies to live and fight on while simultaneously being privileged and debilitated by co-optation, capacitation and complicity in the global neoliberal economy. This concluding chapter presents the women's hopes for the kind of academy they would like to have. It also features poems by other Asian migrant women scholars and activists inviting us to glimpse into snippets of their experiences of migration, racism and womanhood. It ends with the section on a sample of grassroots feminist activisms that are agitating, abolishing and reorganizing existing colonial, racial capitalist and neoliberal structures deeply embedded in the academy and different facets of the global society.

Hope of breaking free from racialization and ornamentalism

Conscripted into an ornamental, supplementary and intermediary role with colonial, racial capitalist labour structure in a white settler-colonial society, the Asian migrant women in contemporary Australian universities I spoke with expressed being done with representation and colonial loads. Not only do they want to be safe and dignified in their existence, but they also want to be allowed to live and thrive without being commodified as a show pony and compelled to self-exoticize and self-racialize their cultural heritage for white gaze, recognition and reward. One respondent put it so eloquently about being permitted to be not that Asian:

I would like to be in a place where I don't have to perform like some big, grateful Asian. I mean, cultural safety is not just being safe to be Asian of some kind or another, but also being safe to not really be that Asian.

Being entrapped in the colonial legacy of racialized power structures means that the women come up against technologies of white supremacy in their everyday reality at the workplace, where they are managed, confined, constricted, censored, appropriated, commodified, rewarded and punished for the elevation and maintenance of white powers. Incredibly and unsurprisingly, some of the respondents related their observations that the chairs of existing academic disciplines on Asian contexts are persistently white people, mostly white men gatekeeping what to be studied and how to study chosen communities. They complained how white men were often employed to lead departments and disciplines on Asian, cultural diversity and race studies, and in some instances, these white men did not even know the languages of the Asian communities they were supposed to be studying and teaching on. The latter also decided and set the benchmarks of how respective disciplines concerning Asian and multicultural communities should look like and invalidated research and scholarships that they did not deem 'legitimate' enough to be included in particular Asian studies disciplines and canon. One respondent wished:

I hope one day, a woman of colour would head this particular centre instead of a white man telling us what is considered research and the canon of Asian studies ... I would like to see more women of colour in the university and head various units especially in non-white areas.

Having said that, several women respondents spoke against the pigeonholding of non-white people in specific area studies and cultural diversity units. While many asked for autonomy and authority to produce research and present multiple, heterogeneous views on specific cultural communities without white gatekeeping, they warned against the danger of being sent into a different kind of enclosure where they were only allowed to do culturally and linguistically diverse works. They protested against being a token hire and representative for diversity tick-box purposes. One respondent repeated her objection of being constrained that way:

> Many women I've talked to know they want to be seen as more than their Asian identity … they want to be afforded the opportunity to explore what they want to explore without that constraint of offering a certain cultural or lived experience perspective … not just be seen as a token representative or token hire but to be treated with dignity that you can be equal contributor to the workplace.

Ultimately, they would like to have real, equitable and meaningful access to career development opportunities like their white colleagues. They ask to be afforded with dignity, full humanity beyond being an ornament in white race-making projects.

Hope of being supported by and colluding with people who get race

An exchange of glances, light nods and eye contacts across the room with another person of colour who is just as agitated by that racist comment, question or suggestion at a staff meeting is enough to validate every fibre of our collective racialized beings and send a booster shot of energy in hope to sustain us till the next destablizing and dehumanizing racialized episode. The women in this study see through the hypocrisy and sinister purposes of corporate diversity, inclusion and equity initiatives and are not bought into the pretentious and tokenistic 'supportive' women leadership, gender equity and cultural diversity programmes that only reinforce existing unequal power structures, maintain coloniality through race, gender and sexuality institutions and serve the interests of white powers. They desire a space untouched, untainted by box-ticking, award-chasing corporate branding exercises where they are not appropriated, ornamentalized and commodified by the colonial, neoliberal university. A respondent desired a safe space where she could share her experiences with other non-white colleagues, listen to their stories and support one another through racialized treatments:

> We need to have a network of non-white academics within the
> university. Maybe a platform where everyone can share their
> experiences, learn from one another, and try to support one another.

Feeling safe enough to be able to share openly about encounters with racism among people of colour is crucial as this respondent indicated:

> I think it would save me a lot of energy, and a lot of time if I could
> just blatantly say things as well. I have to be so careful every time I say
> something.

Another respondent also wished for such a safe space where people would get race without having to teach Race 101, unpack racialization and risk gaslighting:

> I need a safe space for people of colour to talk … that didn't involve
> my white colleagues because I felt if they were there, the space would
> be dominated by them again … they don't realize that sometimes they
> do engage in these much more covert ways of discriminating against
> people of colour colleagues.

This other respondent echoed similar hopes for a judgement-free, gaslighting-proof platform:

> Why aren't we having more chats, like you and I having this one-hour
> chat about racism? Why aren't we having more conversations about
> this and not feel judged and not feel that their experiences are not just
> their perceptions and not feel hurt?

Several women expressed hopes for women of colour feminist mentors and comrades who could provide guidance and support to them whenever they encountered racism in the classroom and other spaces at the workplace and brainstorm together for strategies to fight racism.

Through this study, I came to know of loosely formed, unregulated spaces for people of colour and anti-racism activisms in Australian universities. Some women managed to find themselves such a safe space at the workplace that provided them a refuge and shield albeit momentarily, and one of them shared:

> It's not a formal group or anything but there are people that share my
> politics and my concerns, and so I do feel very culturally safe because
> there are more people like me as well … I feel people have got my back
> … I feel I'm being supported at the moment.

At the point of writing this book, I joined a women of colour network founded by Nida Denson, a fellow Asian migrant woman comrade at our workplace. We emphasize 'women of colour' as an acknowledgement of the women's racialized positions and experiences. We also do so to put forth the network's politicized objectives to counter a colour-blind work environment that wilfully refuses to acknowledge how race continues to operate in systemic, material, relational and individual psychic ways. The loosely formed social network provides a safe social space for any staff and student, woman (cisgender, trans, gender non-binary and genderqueer) of colour who have experienced racialization and minoritization. The network has no formal affiliation with the university's diversity, inclusion and equity initiatives and would like to keep it this way to avoid co-optation and corporatization. The network provides a platform where women of colour could just relax in one other's company, meet for lunch and writing sessions and form supportive friendships at a dominantly white workplace. It is very likely that there are more informal, safe collectives where people of colour employees would gather safely for support and solidarity and not for corporate diversity and inclusion branding, reporting and award application purposes, which I have not yet learned about.

Hope for an anti-colonialism, anti-racism, anti-racial capitalism and anti-neoliberalism academy

The women's narratives have presented ample evidence pointing to the inexistence of a real, meaningful avenue for seeking redress. While there are official complaint management mechanisms where employees and students may use to lodge a complaint about racialized treatments, their stories reveal a series of problems in using such official channels. As evidenced in the women's accounts, the complaint handlers' lack of racial literacy and active de-escalation tactics through whitewashing only saw to the women being slapped with gaslighting and whitesplaining and having their complaints reduced to a matter of cultural and personality differences and, ultimately, dismissed. Some women stated that they would never go near these official complaint mechanisms for fear of facing these additional layers of institutional violence and subsequent retributive effects in their work life and career development. Many hoped that there could be an independent complaint mechanism with no financial contractual relationship with their employer and complaint handlers trained specially in dealing with racism and interrelated discriminatory treatments. A respondent expressed her wish for proper complaint management mechanism where racists are held accountable for their actions. She indicated her displeasure with how white racists could get away so easily without repercussions and punishments:

> I want to see proper mechanisms in place where there are real repercussions for people who commit racism. The cost of committing racial crime is so low at this point in the university.

More importantly, the women desired for a workplace in the academy that is committed to being anti-racist, actively confronting its colonial legacy and ongoing colonial, racial capitalist and neoliberal structures perpetuating injustices and inequalities against Aboriginal and Torres Straits Islander peoples and non-white immigrants and immigrant descendants. They would like to see white power holders at the workplace meaningfully increase the institution's racial literacy, acknowledge the fallacy of so-called meritocracy, abolish existing systems that insist on reinforcing white supremacy and coloniality and reorganize organization's priorities and relationships for the pursuit of racial justice and sustainability. A respondent expressed her hope for an anti-racist framework at the university:

> I think, the University needs to be more openly and fearlessly anti-racist … pursue an anti-racist agenda and it needs to do so meaningfully like,

how do you do that when your VCs, executives and heads of schools are predominantly white men and white women.

Another respondent echoed this similar wish for non-white people driven by an anti-racist ideology and purpose to be in positions of power and decision-making. However, she cautioned against a 'numbers game' approach of just inserting Indigenous and non-white peoples in leadership roles without changing the rules of engagement and organization of power relations:

I'd like to see people who've been traditionally marginalised from academia, whether it is people of colour, Indigenous, Aboriginal, First Nations people, whether it's people who are queer, trans, disabled, neuro divergent, actually making decisions around universities, actually taking leadership and holding power within universities, which would mean that universities or academia as an institution would no longer exist or function the way that it currently exists. It might mean free public education. It might mean open to the community grounded in the community and serving the community rather than essentially operating as a factory, rather than growing the social, symbolic cultural capital for an already economic elite in society … I think that would also require changing the ways that society is organized here because the university is a reflection, microcosm of the racism, the exclusion that Australian society is built around. So it wouldn't be about a body count approach like, oh, look! A dark skin person! Give them power, because, as we know, many of us are all entrenched in the ideologies of white supremacy, colonialism, heteronormativity and so on. So I think it would actually building consciousness, consciousness-raising and solidaristic commitment towards the liberation of all people, especially the most marginalised people.

It is important to note in this respondent's powerful wish that we do not want whitewashing, tokenistic, corporatized Diversity, Inclusion and Equity programmes and other 'inclusive' approaches that concern themselves with representation numbers game and identity politics.

No doubt that seeing more Indigenous peoples and people of colour at a staff retreat, leadership meeting, research seminar and learning and teaching training workshop generates a kind of affective response that helps non-white bodies feel a little more relaxed and safer and less worried and vigilant. No doubt that these Indigenous and people of colour attendees, if allowed and feel safe to speak, bring with them multiple histories, ontologies, epistemes, positionalities, sensibilities and knowledges to destabilize white dominance. One respondent wished for exactly just that:

> First and foremost, it's so hard being in a room full of white faces. It's not just the people. Actually, it's the concepts, the practices. The more people of colour there are in the room, the safer I feel automatically. Alternative ways of thinking and alternative world views that don't feel mechanic. So I think the knowledge that we're allowed to bring into the university can look different … I hope for feeling safe enough to introduce different world views, more training or education around what racism looks like, how to notice it, how your colleagues, when it happens, be supportive, and maybe some more official means to addressing it.

However, many women were clear in stating that by merely increasing numbers and posturing representation, the status quo of unequal power relations would not get disrupted but only reinforced. Straddled with unreasonable representation and colonial loads, the appointed non-white employees, even in leadership positions, only end up being allowed to move within specified colonial, racial capitalist and neoliberal confines, nod to the commands, demands and likes of immediate and broader white powers, and face repercussions should they dare to object. Like what one of the above respondents has indicated, simply increasing the number of non-white bodies at the workplace and up the leadership rung is not useful if they continue to be designated to assume ornamental, representative and supplementary roles and participate in colonial, white race-making projects. One respondent reiterated:

You know, it's not just about having more people of colour in academia. It's about making sure that people are all given equal opportunities and that means people from different genders, racial, class backgrounds are in the mix as well. Which means we also have to think about whose research can be done. Do we need so many academics looking at Europe and North America?

Another respondent also warned against superficially inserting people of colour in leadership positions to signal 'diversity, inclusion and equity' and, consequently, conscripted for neoliberal gains:

> It would be great to just see more people of colour in management. But if they're neoliberal, that's a cannon ball.

A bold examination and revolution of existing power structures within and outside of the academy are what many women in this study urgently hope to happen in the face of the colonial and neoliberal university's direct and complicit implications in devastating global crises of colonialization, imperialism, white supremacy, militarization, global weapon industrial complex, global prison industrial complex, wars, genocides, environmental destructions and the list goes on. A respondent wanted the sector and institution she worked with and, more widely, the host society she has moved into to truthfully acknowledge their culpability and involvements in global racial capitalism and global hierarchy of nations and citizenships, and they were not being benevolent for granting her the rights to stay and work:

> I want to have an equitable workplace where equity is not just the buzzword and you could feel comfortable talking about the impact of colonisation and imperialism on every individual, like the ones that have claimed privilege out of it to people who have been disadvantaged. The reason why I'm in Australia is not just because I came from a shit country with a shit political system. It was also because imperialism and coloniality of power. I've lived through years of sanctions all throughout my life, sanctions that all these Western countries inflicted on me and my family. I've had family members die because of the lack of medications due to sanctions, from cancer, from Covid, from different things. So I'm

not accidentally here. There's been a flow of migration that was extremely political and historical, that has driven people like me here. Now I'm here. I'm bringing in my intellect and hard work. I am supposed to feel like a grateful migrant but I'm not. You know I'm grateful for the things that I've worked really hard for, but I'm not grateful to white saviorism, so my wish is for White Savior to go away even just for one day so that I can feel like I'm sitting here, and I'm cool like with the rest of the people because of my hard work. I wish that our effort of acknowledging racism and coloniality does not get shut down because we've got a long way to go.

Her powerful words spoke so much truth to the white, colonial powers dominating at our workplace.

Anti-colonial, anti-racial capitalist grassroots feminist strategies

I am not only a casualty, I am also a warrior. (Lorde 2019: 30)

I end the book celebrating a few remarkable Asian migrant women feminist comrades and sisters who, to the best of my knowledge, are labouring in fearless, creative and inspirational ways to advance anti-coloniality, anti-racism and grassroots feminist activisms. Some of their works are transnational connecting to communities in their birth countries. This is certainly not an exhaustive list but only a snapshot of the ever-expanding and incredibly powerful collective of Asian migrant women feminist activists shaking colonial grounds for racial justice. I look forward to having readers get in touch with me to share their grassroots anti-racism feminist activism projects and stories on racism in the academy and beyond.

Intan Paramaditha

Intan Paramaditha, Indonesian of Sumatran-Sundanese heritage, anti-colonial feminist academic and writer based in Australia, is one of the co-founders of Sekolah Pemikiran Perempuan (The School of Women's

Thought). Sekolah Pemikiran Perempuan (SPP) sets out to 'situate Third World women as knowing subjects and engage in "epistemic disobedience" to the colonial, capitalist, and heteropatriarchal knowledge system' (SPP 2022). What is inspiring is that SPP, informed by decolonial approach, aims to 'disrupt not through a formal "school" but through guerrilla actions and interventions in various forms of knowledge exchange fora such as classes, lectures, workshops, and broadcasts' (SPP 2022). The organization organizes women living in different islands of Indonesian archipelago and broader Indonesian diaspora to excavate, collect and document their thoughts, knowledges and histories. Primarily, the collective's mission is to centre 'women across cultures, geographical locations and generations' in the Indonesian archipelago and diaspora as 'valid producers of knowledge, challenging the Eurocentric knowledge system and the exclusion of women from local knowledge institutions, such as the state, customs, and religion' (SPP 2022). SPP also releases their manifesto to challenge dominant heteronormative family genealogy and constrictive pathway of 'born-study-work-get married-have children-take care of husband-die' for women in Indonesian society. Instead, SPP's manifesto proposes an anti-colonial feminist understanding of family and a 'practice of living together, without violence, without marginalising people who are deemed different … of care and love, characterised by openness and willingness to adapt, determined by consensus among those who are willing to take part in it' (SPP 2022). SPP wants 'everyone involved [to] have authority over themselves, and believe that a more just future for humans and the universe is something we must absolutely fight for together' (SPP 2022). Besides the groundbreaking, ground-up grassroots anti-coloniality feminism activism with SPP, Intan Paramaditha is actively challenging and breaking down the limits of colonial knowledge production in the literary world and academy. As part of taking an anti-colonial feminist approach in her literary, academic and activism works, Paramaditha (2024) wants to rethink her personal cannon to consider the exemplary works of women of colour in the Global South that often remained hidden, disregarded and erased. The author of *The Wandering*, 'a novel about the condition of ghostliness experienced by travellers and migrants: in between homes, more often homeless, neither nor there', she professes, 'I am not writing alone. I am writing with witches – those who have gone before, those who are brewing, and those who will rise' (Paramaditha 2024). She urges us to rethink our literary influences as a form of 'border crossing: the act of questioning fixed ways of looking, the act of de-naturalising categories, and the act of challenging the boundaries of the self' (Paramaditha 2024). Informed by border thinking and decolonial feminist perspectives, Paramaditha (2024) wants us to actively 'reclaim our literary lineage and stitch a tapestry of defiant voices', 'summon literary witches to traverse, defy erasure, and to borrow from, Gloria Anzaldúa, to rewrite the stories that others have miswritten'.

Israa Merhi

You Are Woman

– Israa Merhi (unpublished, reproduced
with Israa Merhi's permission)

You are woman,
A creature of God,
a wonder sent from the skies,
a precious thing.

You are unique in so many more ways than a human could ever describe. Remember, you are a precious thing.

Don't let the people deceive you.
You pick at your skin like you are planting trenches for them to live in,
your skin is perfect,
don't let them get under it.
Your hair silky smooth or curly locks,
your hair is perfect,

covered or not,
pristine and perfect.

The cloth you wear on your head drags down from generations of
struggle and women of honour, it is perfect.

Whether a woman of children,
working and scrubbing,
walls and windows,
or a woman at an office desk,
or in a classroom,
a construction site or factory floors, you are worthy.

Whether with a child on the way
or four years of trying,
you are worthy.

Whether heartbroken and the feeling of loneliness doesn't leave your
side or newly wedded, you are worthy.

No matter the circumstance,
your feminine energy is a gift.

I know you cry the nights wondering when is relief coming.
You may look at the person you chose and ask yourself,
'Have I ever really been in love with him?'

The words coming from the mouths of strangers or loved ones put
you down because it seems as though no matter how hard you try it is
simply not enough for some, but they are just outside noise.

Back pain and cracked bleeding lines on your hands from working
long shifts don't go unnoticed.
Let me tell you a secret.
You are your child's favourite hero.

You look at other women,
run back to your mirror,
define your worth from what you see in the beauty of others,
but she, the one you desire so much to look like,
has gone and done the same thing as you.

Judged every freckle,
every sunspot,
every new pimple,
every kilo gained on the scale.

She wanted to fit the mould of flawlessness,
until the mould cracked.
Her beauty seeped.
She realised that she would never be good enough to fit the standard.
At last,
she never had to.

Israa Merhi is a poet who has performed her poetry at Bankstown Poetry Slam and published one of her poems, *Generational Ingredients* in Story Factory's *Platform One* journal (Merhi 2023). A second-generation descendant of Lebanese Muslim immigrant family living in Australia, she has written widely on mental health, the search for love and romance and Islam. She has also started focusing her writing and activism on political and humanitarian issues such as the occupation of Palestine. She is a fierce advocate for land to be returned to Indigenous peoples here in Australia and around the world. An aspiring psychology undergraduate student, she hopes to become a clinical psychologist using decolonial and non-oppressive therapeutic approaches. Not only is she a core member of a Palestine Collective organizing activism works alongside academic faculty, she is also the founder of Pro-Palestine student club mobilizing students to demand racial justice and a stop to colonialization of Palestine. She has organized protest rallies, campaign booths, poetry recitations and open letters and is unwavering in her social justice advocacy.

Sukhmani Khorana

Yellow Line

– Sukhmani Khorana
(first published in Ricepaper Magazine, 2016,
reproduced with permission)

We are both in the queue that
says Australian and NZ citizens
where you step across the yellow line and
glance nonchalantly at the camera
while I tentatively put my passport
photo side down and
force a smile that matches
my picture which is also
The image in my head of
a respectable brown woman who is
grateful for the opportunity to
clutch an imprint of the coat of arms as she
steps past the yellow line.

Then on the other side
you breezily put your laptop on the tray and
joke with the man in front of you about
a system that might scan for illegal downloads
While I avoid the gaze of the security officer who
may just stop me for a random check because
such is the privilege of
being able to cross the yellow line.

Sukhmani Khorana, born and grew up in Jammu, India, left her Sikh family home for boarding school in Rajasthan and a brief stint in Delhi before leaving for Adelaide, Australia, for undergraduate and postgraduate studies and, subsequently, Queensland, Wollongong and Sydney for academic job positions. A migrant within her birth country and across oceans, Sukhmani Khorana researches, writes, teaches and engages in activism to improve public understanding of migrants and refugees in the Global North. Author of *Mediated Emotions of Migration* (Khorana 2023) and *The Tastes and Politics of Inter-cultural Food in Australia* (Khorana 2018), Khorana uses interdisciplinary, critical media analytical approaches and creative storytelling methods to document migrants' diverse settlement trajectories. Khorana's anti-coloniality, anti-racism works aim to enact social change through research, advocacy and support of fellow women of colour migrant communities. In the lead up to a national referendum on whether to change the constitution to recognize the First Peoples of Australia by establishing a body called the Aboriginal and Torres Strait Islander Voice, Khorana was one of the key organizers for South Asians for Voice reaching out and encouraging South Asian immigrants to vote yes to an Indigenous voice to Australian parliament (South Asians for Voice 2023).

Helena Liu

Helena Liu migrated from Fuzhou, China, to Sydney, Australia, with her parents when she was five years old. Growing up among immigrant communities in Southwest Sydney, Helena Liu developed a good understanding of migration, racism and settlement based on her lived experiences. As an intersectional feminist academic and activist, Helena Liu set up *Disorient*, a website providing important learning, teaching and research resources on feminisms, intersectionality and activisms. *Disorient* recorded 155,000 visitors from its launch on in November 2020 till its closure in June 2023 (Liu & Taylor 2024). Its mailing list attracted 1,804 subscribers over two years of its operation (Liu & Taylor 2024). *Disorient* project reflects Helena Liu's tireless feminist labour in creating a supportive community for current and former marginalized workers of the academy and sharing generously original reflection workbooks for subscribers to work on internalized oppression and blog posts on topics such as intersectionality theory, introduction to bell hooks and intersectional feminism. In response to feedback from the online community she has developed around *Disorient*, she conducted two online workshops during the global pandemic in 2021 on 'Surviving the white patriarchal academy' and 'Publishing scholarly activist work' (Liu & Taylor 2024). Helena Liu's *Disorient* provided a feminist activist community space and resource hub for a core group of early career academic researchers, community workers, leadership coaches and former university employees who are primarily woman-identifying and marginalized in various ways to seek support, guidance and mentorship. The impact of *Disorient* was also transnational where, for example, 'a Dalit scholarly activist community in India [started visiting the website] from mid-2021', and 'their members began regularly corresponding with Helena via email, offering suggestions for the reading list published on the website, and participating in online workshops' (Liu & Taylor 2024). Even though *Disorient* has closed for now, the intersectional, anti-racist feminist scholarly activist ethics upheld by Helena Liu, author of *Redeeming leadership: An anti-racist feminist intervention* (Liu 2021), are noteworthy.

Souheir Edelbi

Souheir Edelbi, the second-generation descendant of a Lebanese immigrant family in Australia, grew up listening to family stories of migration and anti-Arab, anti-Palestinian racial violence. Seeds of commitment to Palestinian liberation began to sow in Souheir Edelbi at a young age as she learned about the Nakba and oppression faced by Palestinians from her father. Since visiting Palestine in 2010 and bearing witness to the oppression herself, Souheir Edelbi's research, teaching and political activism have been focused on race-making, coloniality and international justice, specifically, Palestinian liberation. Trained in international criminal law with extensive legal professional and human rights advocacy experiences, Souheir Edelbi has worked with human rights organizations supporting the rights of Palestinians and minorities in Iraq and Iran and served on the Advisory Committee of the Racial Justice Centre in Australia. At the point of writing this book, Souheir Edelbi is a co-convenor the Palestine Project at the university she works with as an academic. The Palestine Project seeks to bring together 'academics interested in the connection between pedagogy and current events in Palestine to explore ways in which [they] can support students – and one another – in understanding and responding to current issues of global injustice, in the classroom and beyond' (The Palestine Project 2023). As the co-project convenor, Souheir Edelbi, together with her colleagues, organized a series of advocacy initiatives including introductory reading list on Palestine, pedagogy workshop on talking about Palestine in the classroom, panel discussion on the humanitarian crisis in Gaza and its legal implications and lunchtime talk for student activists to share their Palestine liberation activism on campus experiences.

These incredible Asian migrant women in their respective spheres of influence have been labouring steadfastly for anti-racism, anti-coloniality causes, sometimes fiercely and loudly and other times quietly and strategically. It is important to acknowledge, celebrate and support fellow feminist comrades in going through alternating and contradictory seasons of refusal and compliance, abolition and reproduction, complaint and agreement, and protest and withdrawal. Sara Ahmed (2021) reminds in her book *Complaint!* that not all of us have the resources to complain. We may give ourselves permission to engage with complaint process seasonally whenever we have the capacity to do so. In solidarity with fellow feminist collaborators, may we actively suspend judgement and provide space for one another to do what we need to survive, earn a living, avoid being crushed by the system and preserve finite resources as we collectively persist in our activism works. Undoubtedly, determination in disrupting the workings of monstrous machineries responsible for continual reproduction of elitism, racial capitalism, imperialism and inequalities is crucial. This is why it is also important for feminist collectives to organize themselves in ways where members are permitted to take turns to rest, expunge toxicities that they have taken in at the frontier, nurse injuries, recover and recharge so that they may return to the fight.

Longevity of fire dragon feminism

Since launching Fire Dragon Feminism in the epilogue of my second book (Quah 2020a), I have been asked, 'What is fire dragon feminism?'. In this final note, I would like to address this question first by reiterating what fire dragon feminism is not. Fire dragon feminism is not a self-exoticizing project that seeks to dredge out some ancient mythologies and legends and claim 'authenticity' and 'decoloniality' so as to create an oriental brand that ultimately only excites and delights the white gaze. Fire dragon feminism is not an Asianizing area studies project that insists on essentialist, fixed and contained perspectives in treating Asia as if it needs to and can be made distinct from the rest of the world, where it shares intimate historical and contemporary connections with. Fire dragon feminism is not an ethnocentric project that attempts to elevate Chineseness and Chinese ethno-exceptionalism by summoning the auspicious and powerful cultural meanings of dragon and fire dragon. Fire dragon feminism is not a feminist project that is reserved only for those who share the Chinese horoscope of fire dragon or relate to Chinese zodiac signs and cultural folklores. Fire dragon feminism is also not only relevant to Asian migrant women living and working in white settler-colonial societies.

This particular fire dragon feminism project uses the symbol of fire dragon to explain the ornamental, racialized and sexualized myths imposed on Asian migrant women in settler-colonial and postcolonial societies. Whether it is Fire Dragon, Dragon Lady or Little Dragon Maiden, Asian women have been associated with a range of socially constructed portrayals and expectations, both uplifting and derogatory but nevertheless constrictive. Through speaking at length with Asian migrant women about their experiences with racism in the Australian academy, the project uncovers the workings of racialized myths on Asian migrant women at the workplace and, more broadly, co-constitutive structures of race, gender and sexuality in white settler-colonial societies. Though many of the study's respondents and I were racial majority members of our home societies prior to migration, we immediately found ourselves implicated in the long history of Asian immigration, labour provision, indentureship, racialization and wealth accumulation in white settler-colonial society, as well as dispossession and colonialism of Indigenous peoples. Inheriting this colonial, racial legacy means that we are subject to continuous racialization and conscription as the intermediary between white settler-colonialists and Indigenous peoples, therefore complicit in ongoing colonization of local Indigenous populations. Without doubt, the conditions affect us differently and hence the uneven distribution of life chances, privileges and capital. As bell hooks (2012) instructs, 'indoctrination into dominator thinking in a culture governed by the dictate of imperialist white supremacist capitalist patriarchy is a process that affects all of us to greater and lesser degrees. Understanding dominator thinking heightens the awareness that there is no simple way to identify victims and victimisers, although there are indeed degrees of accountability' (2012: 32). While minoritized migrant subjects face racialization, indoctrination, assimilation and co-optation by imperialist white supremacist capitalist patriarchy, bell hooks (2012) reminds that we need to consider our implications, complicity and accountability in such extractive, life-terminating systems. Reiterating my call made in the earlier chapter, fire dragon feminism calls for minoritized migrant subjects to introspectively reflect upon the colonial legacies and accompanying powers, capital and privileges we have come to inherit and our continuing participation and complicity in the growth of racial capitalism and neoliberalism that persist in dispossessing Indigenous peoples, disenfranchising exploited populations and entrapping us in white race-making projects.

Fire dragon feminism is an ongoing, lifelong, never complete migrant feminist activism that exposes racialized myths imposed on minoritized migrant subjects and archives and activates anti-coloniality, anti-racial capitalism abolitionist and reorganizing strategies. I join fierce and fearless anti-colonial feminist activists to expose the undulating conditions that recruit us to capacitate according to the rules and expectations of those in power, debilitate us simultaneously for such capacitation work, banish us onto the track of debilitation even if we toe the line and fashion ourselves as good migrant citizens and inflict punitive measures of various degrees and sorts should we speak truth to power. I join them to denounce, divest, abolish and revolutionize existing oppressive systems for more sustainable and just futures where we all, not only the elite beneficiaries of colonial, racial capitalist and neoliberal systems, may survive and thrive. This fire dragon feminist over here continues to collude with anti-coloniality, anti-racial capitalism feminist comrades and sisters to flip the master's table, blow flames at life-terminating structures and bring the house down.

Acknowledgements

I would like to express my gratitude to the forty women participants who generously and warmly shared their stories and time with me and permitted their experiences to be discussed in this book. I thank the two reviewers for taking the time to carefully read and provide detailed and highly constructive feedback during the anonymous review process. I would like to thank Yanti Peng for her permission to reproduce her artistic visualization of Fire Dragon Feminism; Beth Yaph for gifting me *Happy Diversity*; Israa Merhi for her permission to publish her unpublished poem *You Are Woman*; Roanna Gonsalves for her permission to reproduce her published poem *What Shall I Wear To Work Today?*; and Sukhmani Khorana for her permission to reproduce her published poem *Yellow Line*. I would also like to thank Intan Paramaditha, Helena Liu, Souheir Edelbi along with Israa Merhi and Sukhmani Khorana for allowing me to showcase their grassroots feminist activisms. I am deeply grateful to my Popo 婆婆, Mummy, Auntie Giok Lan 大姨妈, Auntie Giok Eng 二姨妈, Auntie Geok Buay 姨姨 for sharing their stories and memories with me when I was researching and writing this book. I am indebted to Shawna Tang for sustaining me with unwavering encouragement, lovingly prepared breakfasts, long soul-nourishing walks, and laborious, at times painful (mostly for her), discussions on this book's conceptualization.

References

Abé, R. (2015). Revisiting the dragon princess: Her role in medieval engi stories and their implications in reading the Lotus Sutra. *Japanese Journal of Religious Studies 42*(1): 27–70.

Afro News. (2024). Johns Hopkins medicine employees and students speak out on rebuke of Dr. Sherita Golden by Megan Sayles, 18 January 2024. Available from: https://afro.com/johns-hopkins-medicine-employees-and-students-speak-out-on-rebuke-of-dr-sherita-golden/ (accessed on 15 March 2024).

Ahmed, S. (2012). *On being included: Racism and diversity in institutional life*. Durham, NC: Duke University Press.

Ahmed, S. (2017). *Living a feminist life*. Durham: Duke University Press.

Ahmed, S. (2021). *Complaint!*. Durham, NC: Duke University Press.

Ahmed-Ghosh, H. (ed.) (2015). *Contesting feminisms: Gender and Islam in Asia*. Albany: State University of New York.

Al-Jazeera 101 East (2019). Cambodia's casino gamble. Available from: https://www.aljazeera.com/program/101-east/2019/11/28/cambodias-casino-gamble (accessed on 5 February 2024).

Ang, I. (1996). The curse of the smile: Ambivalence and the 'Asian' woman in Australian multiculturalism. *Feminist Review 52*: 36–49.

Ang, S. (2016). Chinese migrant women as boundary markers in Singapore: Unrespectable, un-middle-class and un-Chinese. *Gender, Place & Culture 23*(12): 1774–87.

Ang, S. (2021). The myth of migrant transience: Racialising new Chinese migrants in mobile Singapore. *Mobilities 16*(2): 236–48.

Ang, S. (2022). *Contesting Chineseness: Nationality, class, gender and new Chinese migrants*. Amsterdam: Amsterdam University Press.

Antwi-Boateng, O. (2017). New world order neo-colonialism: A contextual comparison of contemporary China and European colonization in Africa. *Africology: The Journal of Pan African Studies 10*(2): 177–95.

Anzaldúa, G. (1987). *Borderlands/La Frontera: The new mestiza*. San Franciso: Spinsters/Aunt Lute.

Archer, C., Sison, M., Gaddim, B., & O'Mahony, L. (2022). Bodies of/at work: How women of colour experienced their workplaces and have been expected to 'perform' during the COVID-19 pandemic. *Journal of Intercultural Studies* 43(6): 824–45.

Askarzai, B. (2022). The burqa ban, Islamophobia, and the effects of racial 'othering' in Australian political discourses. *Australian Journal of Politics and History* 68(2): 218–41.

Australian Bureau of Statistics. (2021). *Migration, Australia.* ABS. Available from: https://www.abs.gov.au/statistics/people/population/migration-australia/2019-20 (accessed on 13 February 2024).

Australian Human Rights Commission. (2023). Fact sheet. International day for the elimination of racial discrimination: How 'harmony' hides structural and systemic racism. Available from: https://humanrights.gov.au/our-work/race-discrimination/publications/international-day-eliminat ion-racial-discrimination (accessed on 26 March 2024).

Bagnall, K., & Martinez, J. T. (2021). 'Your government makes us go': The hidden history of Chinese Australian women at a time of anti-Asian immigration laws. *The Conversation*, 14 April 2021. Available from: https:// theconversation.com/your-government-makes-us-go-the-hidden-hist ory-of-chinese-australian-women-at-a-time-of-anti-asian-immigrat ion-laws-154821 (accessed on 10 February 2024).

Baltimore Fishbowl. (2024). Johns Hopkins Medicine chief diversity officer steps down two months after backlash over 'privilege' email by Marcus Dieterle, 5 March 2024. Available from: https://baltimorefishbowl.com/stor ies/johns-hopkins-medicine-chief-diversity-officer-steps-down-two-mon ths-after-backlash-over-privilege-email/ (accessed on 15 March 2024).

Bawany, F. (2021). Multiethnicity in multicultural Singapore: Critical autoethnography to understand racism in Singapore. *Inter-Asia Cultural Studies* 22(1): 118–26.

BBC Chinese. (2001). 中文小说《乌鸦》引起争议. 6 August 2001. Available from: http://news.bbc.co.uk/chinese/simp/hi/newsid_1470000/newsid_ 1476700/1476766.stm (accessed on 22 January 2024).

Besley, T., & Peters, M. A. (2007). Enterprise culture and the rise of the entrepreneurial self. *Counterpoints* 303: 155–74.

Better, S. J. (2008). *Institutional racism: A primer on theory and strategies for social change.* Plymouth, MD: Rowman & Littlefield.

Bhambra, G. K., Gebrial, D., & Nişancıoğlu, K. (eds). (2018). *Decolonising the university*. London: Pluto Press.

Bilge, S. (2013). Intersectionality undone: Saving intersectionality from feminist studies. *Du Bois Review 10*(2): 405–24.

Bilge, S. (2014). Whitening intersectionality: Evanescence of race in intersectionality scholarship. In Wulf D. Hund and Alana Lentin (eds), *Racism and Sociology*, pp. 175–205. London: LIT Verlag.

Blackwell, J. (2024). The government is well behind on Closing the Gap. This is why we needed a Voice to Parliament. *The Conversation*, 13 February 2024. Available from: https://theconversation.com/the-governm ent-is-well-behind-on-closing-the-gap-this-is-why-we-needed-a-voice-to-parliament-223309 (accessed on 16 February 2024).

Bodomo, A. (2018). Is China colonising Africa. In S. Raudino and A. Poletti (eds), *Global economic governance and human development*, pp. 120–33. London: Routledge.

Bong, S. A. (2016). Women's and feminist activism in Southeast Asia. In A. Wong, M. Wickramasinghe, r. hoogland and N. A. Naples (eds), *The Wiley Blackwell encyclopedia of gender and sexuality studies*. Available from: https://doi.org/10.1002/9781118663219.wbegss593 (accessed on 17 January 2024).

Boris, E., & Parreñas, R. (eds). (2010). *Intimate labors: Technologies, cultures and the politics of care*. Stanford, CA: Stanford University Press.

Browning, L., Thompson, K., & Dawson, D. (2013). Women leading research in Australian universities: Are we there yet? In C. Jenkin (ed.), *Ngā reo mō te tika: Voices for equity*, pp. 196–217. Auckland: Equity Practitioners in Higher Education Australasia.

Calabrese, L., & Wang, Y. (2023). Chinese capital, regulatory strength and the BRI: A tale of 'fractured development' in Cambodia. *World Development 169*: 106290. Available from: https://doi.org/10.1016/j.worlddev.2023.106 290 (accessed on 5 February 2024).

Carangio, V., Farquharson, K., Bertone, S., & Rajendran, D. (2021). Racism and white privilege: Highly skilled immigrant women workers in Australia. *Ethnic and Racial Studies 44*(1): 77–96.

Carbin, M., & Edenheim, S. (2013). The intersectional turn: A dream of a common language? *European Journal of Womens Studies 20*(3): 234.

Carrington, K., & Pratt, A. (2003). *How far have we come: Gender disparities in the Australian higher education system*. Canberra: Information and Research Services, Department of the Parliamentary Library Canberra.

Chan, L. L. (2011). Even non-Chinese are falling for the charms of China Dolls. The Star, 21 January 2011. Available from: https://www.thestar.com.my/news/nation/2011/01/21/even-nonchinese-are-falling-for-the-charms-of-china-dolls (accessed on 23 January 2024).

Chang, D. T. (2009). *Women's movements in twentieth-century Taiwan*. Illinois: University of Illinois Press.

Chang, J., Connell, J., Burgess, J., & Travaglione, A. (2014). Gender wage gaps in Australian workplaces: Are policy responses working? *Equality, Diversity and Inclusion 33*(8): 764–75.

Chaudhuri, N. (1994). Memsahibs and their servants in nineteenth century India. *Women's History Review 3*(4): 549–62.

Chen, Y.-C. (2011). *The many dimensions of Chinese feminism*. New York: Palgrave Macmillan.

Cheng, A. A. (2019). *Ornamentalism*. Oxford: Oxford University Press.

Chou, R. S., & Feagin, J. R. (2015). *Myth of the model minority: Asian Americans facing racism*, 2nd edn. New York: Routledge.

Christoffersen, A., & Emejulu, A. (2023). 'Diversity within': The problems with 'intersectional' white feminism in practice. *Social Politics: International Studies in Gender, State & Society 30*(2): 630–53.

Connell, R. (2019). *The good university: What universities actually do and why it's time for radical change*. London: Zed Books.

Collins, P. H. (1990). *Black feminist thought: Knowledge, consciousness and the politics of empowerment*. Boston: Unwin Hyman.

Collins, S. M. (2011). From affirmative action to diversity: Erasing inequality from organisational responsibility. *Critical Sociology 37*(5): 517–20.

Cowlishaw, G. (2004). *Blackfellas, whitefellas, and the hidden injuries of race*. Carlton, Vic: Blackwell.

Crenshaw, K. (1989) Demarginalising the intersection of race and sex: A black feminist critique of antidiscrimination doctrine, feminist theory and antiracist politics, *University of Chicago Legal Forum* (8): 139–67.

David, E. J. R. (ed.). (2014). *Internalised oppression: The psychology of marginalised groups*. New York: Springer.

Davis, A. Y. (1983). *Women, race & class*. New York: Random House USA.

Diverse. (2024). Diversity advocates condemn elimination of DEI staff and programs at University of Florida by Walter Hudson, 3 March 2024. Available from: https://www.diverseeducation.com/leadership-policy/article/15665475/diversity-advocates-condemn-elimination-of-dei-staff-and-programs-at-university-of-florida (accessed on 26 March 2024).

Ee, J. (1961). Chinese migration to Singapore, 1896–1941. *Journal of Southeast Asian History 2*(1): 33–7, 39–51.

Ellingson, L. (2006). Embodied knowledge: Writing researchers' bodies into qualitative health research. *Qualitative Health Research 16*(2): 298–310.

Ellis, C., & Bochner, A. (2000). Autoethnography, personal narrative, reflexivity: Researcher as subject. In Norman K. Denzin and Yvonne S. Lincoln (eds), *Handbook of Qualitative Research*. 2nd edn, 733–768. Thousand Oaks, CA: Sage.

Eng, D., & Han, S. (2018). *Racial melancholia and racial dissociation*. Durham: Duke University Press.

Foroutan, Y., & Mcdonald, P. (2008). Asian migrant women's employment participation: Patterns, determinants and differentials. *Asian Journal of Women's Studies 14*(2): 109–41.

Fujiwara, L., & Roshanravan, S. (eds). (2018). *Asian American feminisms and women of color politics*. Seattle: University of Washington Press.

Gauci, P., Peters, K., O'Reilly, K., & Elmir, R. (2022). The experiences of workplace gendered discrimination for women registered nurses: A qualitative study. *Journal of Advanced Nursing 78*: 1743–54.

Gilbert, E., O'Shea, M., & Duffy, S. (2021). Gender equality mainstreaming and the Australian academy: Paradoxical effects? *Discover Psychology 1*:7.

Gilmore, R. W. (2020). Geographies of racial capitalism. *An Antipode Foundation film*, directed by Kenton Card. Available from: https://antipodeonline.org/geographies-of-racial-capitalism/ (accessed on 2 October 2024).

Goodkind, D. M. (1991). Creating new traditions in modern Chinese populations: Aiming for birth in the Year of the Dragon. *Population and Development Review 17*(4): 663–86.

Gonsalves, R. (2016). *The permanent resident*. Western Australia: University of Western Australia.

Gonsalves, R. (2018). What shall I wear to work today. *Joao-Roque Literary Journal*. 11 August 2018. Available from: https://selma-carvalho.squaresp

ace.com/poetry/2018/8/11/what-shall-i-wear-to-work-today (accessed on 1 May 2024).

Goodkind, D. M. (1991). Creating new traditions in modern Chinese populations: Aiming for birth in the Year of the Dragon. *Population and Development Review* 17(4): 663–86.

Hancock, A.-M. (2011). *Solidarity politics for millennials*. New York: Palgrave Macmillan.

Hartman, S. (2019). *Wayward lives, beautiful experiments: Intimate histories of social upheaval*. New York: W.W. Norton.

Hartman, S. (2022). Craft episode 9: Saidiya Hartman. *Wasafiri: International contemporary writing*, 28 September 2022. Available from: https://www.wasafiri.org/article/craft-episode-9-saidiya-hartman/ (accessed on 1 May 2024).

Haskins, V. (2021). Thomassee: The first Australian ayah. Ayahs and Amahs: Transcolonial servants in Australia and Britain 1780–1945. Project website available from: https://ayahsandAmahs.com/ (accessed on 29 January 2024).

Haskins, V., Banerjee, S., & Lowrie, C. (2021). Ayahs and Amahs: Transcolonial servants in Australia and Britain 1780–1945. Project website available from: https://ayahsandAmahs.com/ (accessed on 29 January 2024).

Heinrich, A. L. (2013). 'A volatile alliance' Queer Sinophone synergies across literature, film, and culture. In H. Chiang and A. L. Heinrich (eds), *Queer Sinophone cultures*, pp. 3–16. London: Routledge.

Henson, B. (2004). Why those China girls worry me. *The Straits Times*, 3 July.

Hickey, S. (2016). 'They say I'm not a typical Blackfella': Experiences of racism and ontological insecurity in urban Australia. *Journal of Sociology* 52(4): 725–40.

Hirshfield, L. E., & Joseph, T. D. (2012). 'We need a woman, we need a black woman': Gender, race, and identity taxation in the academy. *Gender and Education* 24(2): 213–27.

Hochschild, A. R. (2003). Love and gold. In B. Ehrenreich and A. R. Hochschild (eds), *Global woman: Nannies, maids and sex workers in the new economy*, pp. 15–30. New York: Holt/Metropolitan Books.

Holman, J., Tony Adams, S., & Ellis, C. (2013). *The handbook of autoethnography*. Walnut Creek, CA: Left Coast Press.

Hong, C. P. (2020). *Minor feelings: A reckoning on race and the Asian condition*. New York: Random House.

Hong Fincher, L. (2018). *Betraying big brother: The feminist awakening in China*. London: Verso.

hooks, b. (2012). *Writing beyond race: Living theory and practice*. New York: Routledge.

hooks, b. (2015). *Ain't I a woman: Black women and feminism*. New York: Routledge.

Hountondji, P. (ed.). (1997). *Endogenous knowledge: Research trails*. Dakar: Codesria.

Huang, S., & Yeoh, B. S. A. (2005). Transnational families and their children's education: China's 'study mothers' in Singapore. *Global Networks* 5(4): 379–400.

Huang, S., & Yeoh, B. S. A. (2015). Foreign domestic workers in Singapore: A neglected social issue? In D. Chan (ed.), *50 years of social issues in Singapore*, pp. 167–87. Singapore: World Scientific.

Hugo, G., & Harris, K. (2011). *Population distribution effects of migration in Australia*. Report for Department of Immigration and Citizenship. Available from: https://www.homeaffairs.gov.au/research-and-statistics/research/live/migration-australia (accessed on 13 February 2024).

Hutchinson, J., & Eveline, J. (2010). Workplace bullying policy in the Australian public sector: Why has gender been ignored? *Australian Journal of Public Administration* 69(1): 47–60.

Ip, D., & Lever-Tracy, C. (1999). Asian women in business in Australia. In G. A. Kelson and D. L. DeLaet (eds), *Gender and immigration*, pp. 59–81. London: Palgrave.

Jayasuriya, L., & Kee, P. K. (2013). *The Asianisation of Australia? Some facts about the myths*. Melbourne: Melbourne University Press.

Jupp, J. (2007). *From white Australia to woomera*. Cambridge: Cambridge University Press.

Kamanzi, B. (2015). 'Rhodes must fall' – decolonisation symbolism – what is happening at UCT, South Africa? *The Post Colonialist*, 9 April.

Katjasungkana, N., & Wieringa, S. E. (eds). (2012). *The future of Asian feminisms: Confronting fundamentalisms, conflicts and neo-liberalism*. Cambridge: Cambridge Scholars.

Kazanjian, D. (2006). 'When they come here they feal so free': Race and early American studies. *Early American Literature* 41(2): 329–37.

Khatun, S. (2018). *Australianama: The South Asian odyssey in Australia*. St Lucia: University of Queensland Press.

Khorana, S. (2016). Yellow line. *Ricepaper Magazine*, 6 December 2016. Available from: https://ricepapermagazine.ca/2016/12/yellow-line-by-sukhmani-khorana/ (accessed on 1 May 2024).

Khorana, S. (2018). *The tastes and politics of inter-cultural food in Australia*. London: Rowman & Littlefield.

Khorana, S. (2023). *Mediated emotions of migration: Reclaiming affect for agency*. Bristol: Bristol University Press.

Kleven, A. (2019). *Belt and road: Colonialism with Chinese characteristics*. The Lowry Institute. Available from: https://www.lowyinstitute.org/the-interpreter/belt-road-colonialism-chinese-characteristics (accessed from 5 February 2024).

Koleth, E. (2010). *Multiculturalism: A review of Australian policy statements and recent debates in Australia and overseas*. Parliament of Australia, Department of Parliamentary Services, Research Paper No. 6. Available from: https://apo.org.au/sites/default/files/resource-files/2010-10/apo-nid22862.pdf (accessed on 16 February 2024).

Koleth, E. (2015). Multiculturalism at the margins of global Sydney: Cacophonous diversity in Fairfield, Australia. In S. Castles, D. Ozkul & M. Cubas (eds), *Social transformation and migration: National and local experiences in South Korea, Turkey, Mexico and Australia*, pp. 237–54. London: Palgrave.

Kuah, K-E. (1990). Confucian ideology and social engineering in Singapore. *Journal of Contemporary Asia 20*(3): 371–83.

Kwame, N. (1965). *Neo-colonialism: The last stage of imperialism*. London: Thomas Nelson.

Kwon, S. A., & Nguyen, M. T. (2016). Nonprofits, NGOs, and 'community engagement': Refiguring the project of activism in gender and women's studies and ethnic studies. *Scholar & Feminist Online 13*(2). Available from: https://sfonline.barnard.edu/soo-ah-kwon-mimi-thi-nguyen-nonprofits-ngos-and-community-engagement-refiguring-the-project-of-activism-in-gender-and-womens-studies-and-ethnic-studies/ (accessed on 30 March 2024).

Lan, P.-C. (2008). New global politics of reproductive labour: Gendered labour and marriage migration. *Sociology Compass 2*(6): 1801–15.

Latham, J. R. (2017). (Re)making sex: A praxiography of the gender clinic. *Feminist Theory 18*(2): 177–204.

Lentin, A. (2020). *Why race still matters*. Cambridge: Polity Press.

Limpangog, C. P. (2014). Racialised and gendered workplace discrimination: The case of skilled Filipina immigrants in Melbourne, Australia. *Journal of Workplace Rights* 17(2): 191–218.

Liu, H. (2021). *Redeeming leadership: An anti-racist feminist intervention.* Bristol: Bristol University Press.

Liu, H., & Taylor, H. (2024). Making a feminist impact: Mobilising knowledge through scholarly activism. *Equality, Diversity and Inclusion.* Published online first: https://doi.org/10.1108/EDI-07-2023-0240.

Lo, B. (2023). Anti-Asian violence and abolition feminism as Asian American feminist praxis. *Feminist Formations* 35(1): 221–39.

Loomba, A., & Lukose, R. A. (2012). *South Asian feminisms.* Durham: Duke University Press.

Lorde, A. (1988). *A burst of light and other essays.* Michigan: Firebrand Books.

Lorde, A. (2019). *Sister outsider.* Great Britain: Penguin Random House.

Lowe, L. (2015). *The intimacies of four corners.* Durham: Duke University Press.

Lowrie, C. (2021). Chinese Amahs in Britain and Australia. Ayahs and Amahs: Transcolonial servants in Australia and Britain 1780–1945. Project website available from: https://ayahsandAmahs.com/ (accessed on 29 January 2024).

Loy-Wilson, S. (2014). New directions in Chinese-Australian history. *History Australia* 11(3): 233–8.

Loy-Wilson, S. (2019). Trouble in white Australia: Marilyn Lake, Australian history and Asian exclusion. In Joy Damousi and Judith Smart (eds), *Contesting Australian history: Essays in honour of Marilyn Lake*, pp. 175–89. Melbourne: Monash University.

Lyons, L. (2004). *A state of ambivalence: The feminist movement in Singapore.* Boston: Brill.

Ma Rhea, Z. (1998). Production, reproduction and dissemination of the idea of 'white' superiority: A study of an academically-generated ideas in the universities of the empire and Commonwealth. Unpublished paper.

Mbembe, A. J. (2016). Decolonising the university: New directions. *Arts and Humanities in Higher Education* 15(1): 29–45.

Mellor, D. (2006). The experiences of Vietnamese in Australia: The racist tradition continues. *Journal of Ethnic and Migration Studies* 30(4): 631–58.

Meng, Q. 孟青, & Chen, X. 陈欣 (2006). 中国女性在东南亚名声受损 小龙女成卖淫代名词. 环球时报, 25 December 2006. Available from: https://

news.sina.cn/sa/2006-12-25/detail-ikknscsk1560197.d.html (accessed on 22 January 2024).

Merani, K., & Gonsalves, R. (2019). How Indian servants brought to Australia lived and survived in the 19th century. SBS Hindi podcast available from: https://www.sbs.com.au/language/hindi/en/podcast-episode/how-indian-servants-brought-to-australia-lived-and-survived-in-the-19th-cent ury/9s934v1e4 (accessed on 11 February 2024).

Merhi, I. (2023). Generational ingredients. *Platform Issue 1*. Story Factory. Available from: https://allthebestradio.com/featured/566-platform-story-factory/ (accessed on 1 May 2024).

Merhi, I. (unpublished). *You are woman.*

Meronek, T., & Major, M. (2023). *Miss Major: Conversations with a black trans revolutionary*. London: Verso.

Mohanty, C. T. (2003). *Feminism without borders: Decolonising theory, practising solidarity*. Durham, NC: Duke University Press.

Mohanty, C. T. (2013). Transnational feminist crossings: On neoliberalism and radical critique. *Signs: Journal of Women in Culture and Society* *38*(4): 967–91.

Mok, T. M. (2022). Black Asian, white Asian: Racial histories and East Asian choices in the white settler states. In A. Tecun, L. Lopesi and A. Sankar (eds) *Towards a grammar of race in Aotearoa New Zealand*. Wellington: Bridget Williams Books.

Moodie, D., Menzel, K., Cameron, L., & Moodie, N. (2022). Blak & salty: Aboriginal women reflect on lateral violence & racism in Australian universities. In E. Lee and J. Evans (eds), *Indigenous women's voices: 20 years on from Linda Tuhiwai Smith's Decolonizing Methodologies*, pp. 69–85. London: Zed Books.

Moran, C. (2022). 'African kids can': Challenging the African gangs narrative on social media. *Media International Australia*. First published online: https://doi.org/10.1177/1329878X221142879.

Moreton-Robinson, A. (2020a). *Talkin' up the white woman: Aboriginal women and feminism*. St Lucia: University of Queensland Press.

Moreton-Robinson, A. (2020b). I still call Australia home: Indigenous belonging and place in a white postcolonising society. In S. Ahmed, C. Castañeda, A.-M. Fortier and M. Sheller (eds) *Uprootings/regroupings: Questions of home and migration*, 23–40. London: Routledge.

Morris, B. (1989). *Domesticating resistance: The Dhan-Gadi Aborigines and the Australian state*. London: Routledge.

Morrison, T. (1975). A humanist view. Speech at Portland State University's Oregon Public Speakers' collection: Black studies center. Public Dialogue on 30 May 1975. Available from: https://www.mackenzian.com/wp-content/uploads/2014/07/Transcript_PortlandState_TMorrison.pdf (accessed 21 May 2022).

Murji, K. (2007). Sociological engagements: Institutional racism and beyond. *Sociology 41*(5): 843–55.

Murphy, P., O'Brien, B., & Watson, S. (2003). Selling Australia, selling Sydney: The ambivalent politics of entrepreneurial multiculturalism. *Journal of International Migration and Integration 4*(4): 471–98.

Nash, J. (2016). Feminist originalism: Intersectionality and the politics of reading. *Feminist Theory 17*(1): 3–20.

Nash, J. (2019a). *Black feminism reimagined: After intersectionality*. Durham, London: Duke University Press.

Nash, J. (2019b). Pedagogies of desire. *Differences 30*(1): 198–217.

Nash, M., & Moore, R. (2020). 'Death by a thousand cuts': Women of colour in science face a subtly hostile work environment. *The Conversation*, 11 February 2020.

New South Wales (NSW). (2024). Commemorative birth certificates. Available from: https://www.nsw.gov.au/family-and-relationships/births/commemorative-birth-certificates (accessed on 20 February 2024).

New York Post. (2024). Johns Hopkins chief diversity officer steps down months after calling men, white people 'privileged' by Alyssa Guzman, 6 March 2024. Available from: https://nypost.com/2024/03/06/us-news/johns-hopkins-chief-diversity-officer-steps-down-months-after-privilege-list-blowout/ (accessed on 15 March 2024).

Ng, C., Mohammad, M., & Tan, B. H. (2006). *Feminism and the women's movement in Malaysia: The unsung (r)evolution*. Abingdon, NY: Routledge.

Ngo, H. (2019). 'Get over it'? Racialised temporalities and body orientations in time. *Journal of Intercultural Studies 40*(2): 239–53.

Paramaditha, I. (2024). Summoning literary witches: Intan Paramaditha rethinks her personal canon. *Literary Hub*, 25 March 2024. Available from: https://lithub.com/summoning-literary-witches-intan-paramaditha-rethinks-her-personal-canon/ (accessed on 9 May 2024).

Park, J. (2019). Embodied inter-referencing: Encounters with and among 'Asian' students in the Australian classroom. *Inter-Asia Cultural Studies* 20(2): 271–89.

Parreñas, R. S. (2014). The intimate labour of transnational communication. *Families, Relationships and Societies 3*(3): 425–42.

Pearson, L. (2023). The truth about Harmony Day. *IndigenousX*, 21 March 2023. Available from: https://indigenousx.com.au/the-truth-about-harm ony-day/ (accessed on 26 March 2024).

Peters, M. A. (2007). Neoliberalism, education, and the crisis of Western capitalism. *Policy Futures in Education 48*(2): 85–102.

Pheterson, G. (1986). Alliances between women: Overcoming internalised oppression and internalised domination. *Journal of Women in Culture and Society 12*(1): 146–60.

Prasso, S. (2005). *The Asian mystique: Dragon ladies, geisha girls, and our fantasies of the exotic Orient.* New York: Public Affairs.

Preciado, P. (2013). *Testo Junkie: Sex, Drugs, and Biopolitics in the Pharmacopornographic Era* (trans. Benderson B). New York: Feminist Press.

Preciado, P. (2020). In conversation with Paul Preciado, interview by Guy Mackinnon-Little. Tank Magazine Issue 82. Available from: https://magaz ine.tank.tv/issue-82/talks/paul-b-preciado (accessed on 8 March 2024).

Puar, J. K. (2011). 'I would rather be a cyborg than a goddess': Intersectionality, assemblage, and affective politics'. *philoSOPHIA 2*(1): 49–66.

Puar, J. K. (2017). *The right to Maim: Debility, capacity, disability.* Durham: Duke University Press.

Quah, E. L. (2020a). *Transnational divorce: Understanding intimacies and inequalities from Singapore.* London: Routledge.

Quah, E. L. (2020b). Navigating emotions at the site of racism: Feminist rage, queer pessimism and fire dragon feminism. *Australian Feminist Studies* 35(105): 203–16.

Quah, E. L., (2023). Gender and Power. *Sydney Review of Book*, Writing Gender Series. Available from: https://sydneyreviewofbooks.com/essay/ gender-and-power/ (accessed on 20 February 2024).

Quah, E. L., & Ridgway, A. (2021). The woman writer's body: Multiplicity, neoliberalism and feminist resistance. *Gender, Work & Organisation 29*(1): 44–57.

Quah, E. L. & Tang, S. (2024). Racialised queer Chinese migrants in Australia: Entanglements of queerness and Chineseness. *Journal of Intercultural Studies*. Published Online First: https://doi.org/10.1080/07256 868.2024.2382747.

Radhakrishnan, S., & Solari, C. (2015). Empowered women, failed patriarchs: Neoliberalism and global gender anxieties. *Sociology Compass* 9(9): 784–802.

Risberg, P. (2019). The give-and-take of BRI in Africa. *New Perspectives in Foreign Policy 17*: 43–7.

Robinson, C. (2021). *Black Marxism*, revised and updated 3rd edn. Chapel Hill: University of North Carolina Press.

Robson, P., & Walter, T. (2013). Hierarchies of loss: A critique of disenfranchised grief. *Journal of Death and Dying 66*(2): 97–119.

Roces, M., & Edwards, L. P. (2010). *Women's movements in Asia: Feminisms and transnational activism*. Abingdon: Routledge.

Roy, S. (2012) *New South Asian feminisms: Paradoxes and possibilities*. London: Zed.

Saw, S-H. (2012). *The population of Singapore*, 3rd edn. Singapore: ISEAS.

Sekolah Pemikiran Perempuan (SPP). (2022). About us. Manifesto. Available from: https://www.pemikiranperempuan.org/ (accessed on 6 May 2024).

Sen, I. (2009). Colonial domesticities, contentious interactions: Ayahs, wet-nurses and memsahibs in colonial India. *Indian Journal of Gender Studies 16*(3): 299–328.

Shah, S. (1997). *Dragon ladies: Asian American feminists breathe fire*. Boston, Brooklyn: South End Press.

Shi, X. (2010). Women, international migration and development: Chinese women's migration to Southeast Asia since 1978. *International Journal of China Studies 1*(1): 216–29.

Smith, G., & Wesley-Smith, T. (eds). (2021). *The China alternative: Changing regional order in the Pacific*. Acton: Australian National University Press.

South Asians for Voice. (2023). About us. Available from: https://southasiansf orvoice.org/ (accessed on 6 May 2024).

Sriprakash, A., Rudolph, S., & Gerrard, J. (2022). *Learning whiteness: Education and the settler colonial state*. London: Pluto Press.

Statistics Singapore. (2021). *Census of population 2020: Demographic characteristics, education, language and religion*. Available from: https://

www.singstat.gov.sg/-/media/files/publications/cop2020/sr1/cop2020sr1.pdf (accessed on 12 February 2024)

Stephenson, P. (2003). New cultural scripts: Exploring the dialogue between indigenous and 'Asian' Australians. *Journal of Australian Studies* *27*(77): 57–68.

Tan, P. L. (2023). *Superstitions on Tiger or Dragon year babies won't disappear, but they will evolve*. Singapore: Global-Is-Asian, Lee Kuan Yew School of Public Policy. Available from: https://lkyspp.nus.edu.sg/gia/article/superstitions-on-tiger-or-dragon-year-babies-won-t-disappear-but-they-will-evolve (accessed on 12 February 2024).

Tappe O., & Rowedder, S. (eds). (2023). *Extracting development: Contested resource frontiers in mainland Southeast Asia*. Singapore: ISEAS–Yusof Ishak Institute.

Tehrani, N. (2015). Why is my curriculum white. *Occupied Times*, 27 August 2015. Available from: https://theoccupiedtimes.org/?p=14056 (accessed on 12 February 2024).

The Palestine Project. (2023). The Palestine Project. Available from: https://www.westernsydney.edu.au/schools/sol/palestine-project (accessed on 12 May 2024).

Trinh, T. M. H. (1989). *Woman, native, other: Writing postcoloniality and feminism*. Bloomington: Indiana University Press.

Tuck, E., &, Yang, K. W. (2012). Decolonisation is not a Metaphor. *Decolonisation: Indigeneity, Education & Society 1*(1): 1–40.

Twomey, C. (2023). Amah activism: Domestic servants and decolonisation in 1960s Malaysia and Singapore. *International Labour and Working-Class History 103*: 312–27.

United Nations Statistics Division. (2024). Methodology: Standard country or area coded for statistical use. Available from: https://unstats.un.org/unsd/methodology/m49/ (accessed on 6 January 2024).

Wang, Z. (2014). The Chinese dream: Concept and context. *Journal of Chinese Political Science 19*: 1–13.

Watego, C. (2021). *Another day in the colony*. St Lucia: University of Queensland Press.

Whyman, T., Murrup-Stewart, C., Young, M., Carter, A., & Jobson, L. (2021). 'Lateral violence stems from the colonial system': Settler-colonialism and lateral violence in Aboriginal Australians. *Postcolonial Studies 26*(2): 183–201.

Winchester, H. P. M., & Browning, L. (2015). Gender equality in academia: A critical reflection. *Journal of Higher Education Policy and Management 37*(3): 269–81.

Women of Colour Australia. (2021). *Women of Colour Australia Workplace Survey Report 2021*. Available from: https://womenofcolour.org.au/wp-content/uploads/2022/02/WOMEN-OF-COLOUR-AUSTRALIA-WORKPLACE-SURVEY-REPORT-2020-2021.pdf (accessed on 24 July 2022).

Yaph, B. (unpublished). *Happy Diversity*.

Yaph, B. (2015). *Eat first, talk later*. Sydney: Penguin Random House.

Yaph, B. (2017). *The red pearl and other stories*. Sydney: Vagabond Press.

Yeoh, B. S. A., & Huang, S. (2010). Sexualised politics of proximities among female transnational migrants in Singapore. *Population, Space & Place 16*: 37–49.

Yeoh, B. S. A., & Lin, W. (2013). Chinese migration to Singapore: Discourses and discontents in a globalising nation-state. *Asian and Pacific Migration Journal 22*(1): 31–54.

Yoong, M., & Lee, S. (2023). 'China doll snatched away my husband': The intersectional othering of Chinese migrant women in a Malaysian newspaper. *Discourse, Context & Media 54* (August 2023), published online: https://doi.org/10.1016/j.dcm.2023.100713.

Yuval-Davis, N. (2012). Dialogical epistemology: An intersectional resistance to the 'Oppression Olympics'. *Gender & Society 26*(1): 46–54.

Yuval-Davis, N. (2013). *A situated intersectional everyday approach to the study of bordering*. Working Paper 2. Brussels: European Commission EU Borderscapes.

Zheng, X.-Y. 鄭筱筠. (1997). 印度佛典那伽故事與中國龍王龍女故事. Unpublished thesis. Shanghai: Fudan University. Available from: https://buddhism.lib.ntu.edu.tw/DLMBS/en/search/search_detail.jsp?seq=126431 (accessed on 21 January 2024).

Index